DEMARXIFICATION

SIMPLE VISUAL FORMULAS FOR
COMBATING SOCIALIST INDOCTRINATION

An Introduction to the Educational Program by

LISA RAHON

Published by:

All rights reserved. No part of this publication may be reproduced, distributed, or transmitted in any form or by any means—including photocopying, recording, or other electronic or mechanical methods—without the prior written permission of the author, except in the case of uses permitted by copyright law. Although the author and publisher have made every effort to ensure that the information in this book was correct at press time, they do not assume and hereby disclaim any liability to any party for any loss, damage, or disruption caused by errors or omissions, whether such errors or omissions result from negligence, accident, or any other cause.

Adherence to applicable laws and regulations, including international, federal, state, and local governing professional licensing, business practices, advertising, and all other aspects of doing business in the U.S., Canada, or any other jurisdiction is the sole responsibility of the reader and consumer.

Neither the author nor the publisher assumes any responsibility or liability on behalf of the consumer or reader. Any perceived slight of specific individuals or organizations is purely constructive criticism intended to provide feedback for improvement.

This publication contains brief quotations, excerpts, and certain images that are either in the public domain or used under the doctrine of "fair use" (17 U.S.C. § 107) for purposes of commentary, criticism, education, and research. Every effort has been made to credit original authors and sources in the endnotes and references.

All illustrations in this book, whether hand-drawn or created with AI assistance, are original works produced or adapted by the author. They are included for educational and historical purposes only and are not intended as photographic likenesses or endorsements.

Some images in this book were created with the assistance of AI tools and subsequently edited and customized by the author.

Scripture quotations taken from *The Holy Bible, New International Version® NIV®*
Copyright © 1973, 1978, 1984, 2011 by Biblica, Inc. Used with permission. All rights reserved worldwide.

Contents—The formulas in each section below serve as visual aids for classrooms, lecture halls, or independent study. They may be drawn on a chalkboard or printed as handouts. Although the formulas function individually or in combination, the full matrix is the ideal tool for discussion and debate.

A BRIEF HISTORY
An Introduction to the Topic..page 2

Section 1

FORMULA 1A
Appreciating Freedom, Rejecting Corruption ....page 12

FORMULA 1B
The False Narrative of the "Oppressed" vs. the "Oppressor" ....page 26

FORMULA 1C
Levels of Corruption..page 34

Section 2

FORMULA 2A
How Marxism Destroys ....page 38

FORMULA 2B
"Enter Through the Narrow Gate…" ....page 50

FORMULA 2C
Taxpayer Choice & Privatization..page 62

Section 3

FORMULA 3A
Weapons of Mass Distraction..page 72

FORMULA 3B
Offending the Few vs. Harming Everyone.....................................page 75

FORMULA 3C
Spinning Our Wheels—Pros, Cons & Missed Opportunities ....page 77

Section 4

ANCILLARY FORMULAS
Tools for Exposing & Dismantling Marxist Nonsense.........................page 84

SUMMARY—THE FULL DEMARXIFICATION MATRIX
How the Formulas Work Together...page 88

SOME SOLUTIONS ....page 90

ENDNOTES/REFERENCE ....page 92

THE LAST WORD ....page 96

We find ourselves in a battle between truth and nonsense—between the world's innocent families seeking a prosperous life—and powerful, corrupt individuals seeking the subjugation of others. It's a conflict between independent thinkers and those who angrily defend mainstream narratives—even when those narratives defy truth, common sense, and decency.

In recent years, media, academia, and other institutions have shown us just how much power they wield. In the U.S., they have fueled unprecedented levels of hatred, tearing apart families, friendships, and communities like never before. The tools they employ to accomplish this are rooted in the principles of *Marxism*.[1]

They demonize the United States, its history, and its majority populations. They promote government control (socialism) over individual freedom (capitalism). Almost every demographic group is pitted against another. They flip morality—calling good bad, bad good, and treating truth and decency as the enemy.

But these demonizations and divisions are exaggerated—if not outright manufactured.

Our true enemies are not *each other*, but the power-hungry individuals who manufacture and weaponize these narratives to divide and control the rest of us.

History confirms this. Humanity's worst miseries—wars, genocide, mass subjugation—do not originate from populations seeking better lives, but almost always from the corrupt powerful few.

Yet, instead of uniting against these individuals, Americans allow them to turn us against each other—and against our great country.

The rights and freedoms we enjoy in the United States are singular in human history, granting ordinary people unprecedented opportunities and freedoms. Yet, for decades, American students have been taught to disdain the United States.

Yes, a covert war has been waged against our country for generations—not on the battlefield, but in classrooms and lecture halls.

Academia is rife with Marxist inversions of morality and reality: "Kids can choose their gender,"[2] "The U.S. is racist," "Fathers are unnecessary," and so on *ad nauseam*.

Year after year, graduates carry these destructive narratives into our institutions, industries, and ultimately our collective consciousness. Today, Marxist inversions permeate nearly every corner of our society.

Some years ago, I started to notice patterns in these narratives.

Stunned by the number of otherwise good people deceived into hating their fellow Americans, I decided to act. Drawing on my experience as an art director and graphic designer, I began crafting simple formulas that illustrate these patterns.

Using the formulas in discussion and debate clarifies the importance of freedom, truth, and traditional Judeo-Christian values. At the same time, they expose Marxist psychological tactics in a way that is easy to remember and difficult to deny.

Old-school imperialists roll across borders with tanks and guns. Marxists roll across institutions with destructive ideas cloaked in virtue-laced slogans.

Understanding Marxism's insidious patterns can require hours of study. The formulas in *DeMarxification* expose those patterns in minutes.

Armed with this clarity, anyone can confidently debate socialist indoctrination wherever it rears its ugly head—in classrooms, boardrooms, or newsrooms.

In decades past, children were taught to blindly trust our institutions. Today, we must teach skepticism. It is our duty to prepare young people for the reality we once hoped to spare them from: many in government, media, and academia have agendas opposed to their well-being.

Young people must think for themselves, seek out the facts, recognize empty demonization and deception—and reject the institutions that depend on these tactics.

Thank you for your interest. I hope you enjoy the program.

Sincerely,

Lisa Rahom

A Brief History

From news panels to dinner tables, the term *Marxism* keeps popping up. But many individuals have only a vague idea of what it is or how it works. The following pages provide a basic historical background for those whose education failed to include the history of an ideology that has so shaped the world we live in today.

Imperialism, Capitalism, and Marxism: Humanity's Journey from Monarchs to Markets to Manifestos. (Formula 1A, page 12)

IMPERIALISM—Right-Wing Subjugation:

For most of mankind's existence, the rights and individual freedoms that we cherish today were scarcely known. It was all about kings and queens, emperors and warlords ruling over the masses. In most of the world, bloodlines ruled—they lived in opulence; the masses lived as peasants.

But in the late 18th century, American patriots in the thirteen colonies fought back and achieved the first successful mass uprising that proclaimed freedom was *endowed by their Creator*[3]—not endowed by a king or emperor.

These brave revolutionaries faced the mighty British Empire, armed with nothing but muskets and determination. After much bloodshed, they sent the redcoats packing and declared the colonies to be an independent country: *the United States of America*.

Although the word "capitalism" was not yet in use, the Boston Tea Party[4] and the American Revolution were about breaking away from imperialism and unfair taxation.

CAPITALISM—Economic Freedom:

Over time, another revolution—the Industrial Revolution[5]—would deal the death blow to aristocracy in many parts of the world. In Europe, for instance, transportation improved,[6] and workers gained options for employment. They were no longer captive to local lords because they could take a train to any number of places for factory jobs and other work. Today, imperialist castles stand in ruins; butlers and footmen are a thing of the past.[7]

It's true—many early factory owners exploited workers and could be described as "new imperialists." Some even purchased aristocratic titles.[8] But the spread of entrepreneurship to anyone with ambition couldn't be stopped—and in the end, it was *capitalism*—open competition for workers and customers—that ultimately forced the entire system toward fairness, creating what we now take for granted as a *middle class*.

Societies built on this economic freedom have consistently produced the greatest prosperity for the greatest number of people.[9] In the U.S., even our poorest individuals live better than the vast majority of the world's population.[10]

Let's not forget that these comforts and freedoms are precious gifts that must be protected, because—sadly—there will always be individuals who seek to subjugate others.

And since Americans are both heavily armed[11] and unimpressed by bloodlines, today's tyrants have had to employ covert methods for subjugating populations...

MARXISM—Left-Wing Subjugation:

In recent centuries, corrupt individuals have employed a psychological approach to manipulate populations. Their weapon of choice is *Marxism*—the root ideology on which *socialism* and *communism* are based.[12] This ideology has saturated the American left—so-called "liberals"—who today are anything but liberal.[13]

Marxism is an insidious ideology popularized by Karl Marx and Friedrich Engels in *The Communist Manifesto*.[14] Whether by ignorance or intent, this poorly written manifesto presents only two options—*imperialism* or *Marxism*—while vilifying the natural state of thriving human society: economic freedom, referred to today as "capitalism." *(page 25)*

It was Karl Marx himself who promoted the use of the negative-sounding term "capitalism" with his book, *Das Kapital*.[15] This term allows economic freedom to be demonized, and conflated with imperialism. Orwell nailed it in *1984*[16] with the tyrannical Party's slogan: *"FREEDOM IS SLAVERY."* *(page 16)*

As alien as it sounds to decent people, the goal of Marxism is the *tearing down of society*[17] to supposedly be "built back better"[18] as a workers' "utopia."

As illustrated in the formulas, the tearing down is done in several ways.

One is by dividing populations using Marx's model.

"Oppressed" vs. "Oppressor"

Marx's original theory cast factory owners (the bourgeoisie) as the villainous oppressors and workers (the proletariat) as the oppressed victims, with the government seizure of production as the alleged solution. *(Formula 1B, page 26)*

Again, in Marx's day, some factory owners were behaving like corrupt imperialists, but Marx and Engels' solution, "the centralization of all instruments of production in the hands of the state," under the misleading slogan "Workers of the world, unite!"[19] merely replaced the tyranny of wealth with the tyranny of the state.

The seizure of private enterprise not only destroys business owners but also dooms workers. It strips them of employment options, the leverage that competition creates, and the potential to ever own a business themselves. In the end, it returns populations to a form of subjugation often worse than historic imperialism—while government elites live like the very monarchs they claim to oppose.

In Marxist societies, ambition survives, but only in utter corruption—often known as the *black market*—where only those in bed with corrupt officials can do business; everyone else risks execution for engaging in trade. Orwell nailed it again in *Animal Farm:* under enforced "equity," some end up "more equal than others."[20]

Where Marxist leadership promised "utopia"—populations experienced famine, executions, gulags, and neighbor-against-neighbor betrayal—making the injustices of the castle-dwellers look mild by comparison.

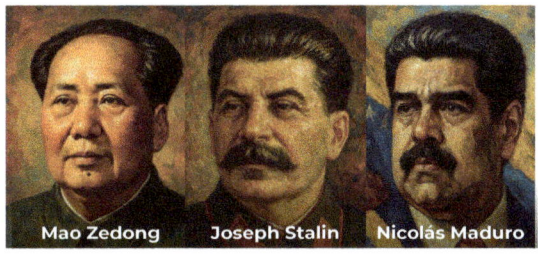
Mao Zedong Joseph Stalin Nicolás Maduro

Totalitarian dictators such as Mao Zedong, Joseph Stalin, and, more recently, the Chávez–Maduro regime subjugated populations on behalf of "the people" they were supposed to represent.

Marxist-based systems—from the Bolshevik Revolution[21] to the "Great Leap Forward"[22] to the devastating collapse of once-thriving Venezuela[23]—caused an estimated 100 million deaths and inflicted horrific suffering on more than a billion. At the same time, capitalist societies were thriving.

One would think that Marx's childish theory would be abandoned, and societies would take up the free-market formula for success. But instead, devotees of Marxism and their "useful idiots" push on.

"Equity"

Another weapon of Marxism is the childish notion of "equity"—the attempt to impose the utopian vision of *equal outcomes* across society.[24]

This allegedly noble ideal—framed as "taking from the rich to give to the poor," or again, "Workers of the world, unite!"—misleads the well-intentioned into thinking they're fighting for the downtrodden, when in fact they're fueling tyranny.

"Equity" is unnatural and unfair: I don't deserve the salary of a brain surgeon; a teenage cashier doesn't deserve my income. Do you want a brain surgeon who is paid the same as a teenage cashier? North Korean defector Yeonmi Park recounts how doctors in her homeland were paid less than a dollar a month.[25] She risked her life to escape that brutal regime, endured heinous exploitation in China, and finally reached the "bastion of freedom"—*Columbia University*—only to be horrified to find professors enforcing the very ideology she had risked death to escape.[26]

NEO-MARXISM—Marxism on Steroids

In times past, imperialists sat on thrones and took territory with weapons. Today, Marxists sit in faculty lounges and take higher education with weaponized ideas.[27]

Only college students and others with little real-world experience could believe that "equity" is fair—or that government control of *anything*, let alone *everything*, ever works.

Graduates then quietly colonize institutions, industries, media, and culture. Imperialists tend to play the short game; Marxists are content even if their plans take generations to unfold—referred to as the "long march through the institutions."[28]

Neo-Marxism is Marxism on steroids: the application of this "oppressed versus oppressor" narrative to every nook and cranny of Western society.

While Marxism masquerades as a movement for the workers and against the business owners, neo-Marxism masquerades as movements for any group and against any other group, whether they are genuinely in opposition or not.

As the formulas illustrate, all forms of Marxism will harm the groups they claim to help, as well as the groups they dub "oppressors." All rely on ignorance and compliance of populations. All serve the interests of centralized authorities at the expense of the general populations.

Although Marxism was causing real damage in places around the world for almost a century, the U.S. remained somewhat (but not completely) unscathed by Marxist proponents and influences. This was not to last.

In 1935, a group of neo-Marxists—the Frankfurt School[29]—fled Hitler's Germany and sought refuge in the U.S. And instead of thanking Americans for their protection, these academics spent the next three decades scheming to dismantle Western culture through our higher educational system.

Marcuse, Adorno, Horkheimer, and earlier proponents of Marxism believed that in order to establish a communist utopia, it was necessary to subvert Western culture, Christianity, traditional families and the United States. These tactics follow patterns that are exposed by the formulas in this book.

Today, the "long march" is complete. A recent survey of Harvard's Faculty of Arts and Sciences revealed that more than 77 percent of faculty identified as "liberal" or "very liberal," while only 2 percent described themselves as conservative.[30]

Frighteningly, today—as a result of this institutional left-wing saturation—62 percent of Americans aged 18–29[31] say they hold a "favorable view" of *socialism*: the on-ramp to history's deadliest ideology. Countless others, knowingly or not, support Marxist movements. ANTIFA, Black

Lives Matter, and LGBT Pride openly use the socialist fist in their logos and signs; BLM leaders boast that they are "trained Marxists,"[32] and celebrities like Sean Penn defend socialist dictators.[33]

Often, those who praise socialism cannot even define it. When asked, they sputter, parrot Marxist clichés, credit socialism for benefits only capitalism produces, or literally flee the scene.

Marx pitted *factory owners* against *workers*—destroying both in the process. As shown in the formulas, today's Marxist-influenced left pits nearly every group against another—Blacks vs. Whites, women vs. men, LGBT vs. straight, vaxxed vs. unvaxxed, left vs. right—even Girl Scouts vs. Boy Scouts.

These divisions are far too thorough to be accidental, and in true Marxist fashion, they ultimately harm both groups.

In addition to dividing populations, Marxism is designed to make its followers side *with* the immoral and destructive—and *against* the wholesome and beneficial—while tragically believing themselves the epitome of virtue. *(Formula 2A, page 38)*

Also shown in the formulas, Marx's framework—through Hollywood and other institutions—is used today to harm Americans. They glamorize casual sex, crime, and drug use while unfairly demonizing law enforcement,[34] wholesome behavior, Christian family values, and being a good student.[35] The result is the moral train wreck America has become.

Beyond Hollywood, Marxist-influenced professors shame students into following *groupthink*.[36] The result is infantilization: students no longer discern right from wrong *on their own,* but angrily defend whatever the group consensus appears to be—even when the idea is harmful or ridiculous. *(Formula 3A, page 72)*

Mainstream media and academia not only sow division and promote destructive behavior—they divert the energy of potential reformers toward the manufactured "outrage of the week," while existential problems are ignored.

Today, young and old can be seen protesting their own freedoms, clamoring for their own subjugation, and demanding rights they already have—all while society crumbles around us.

Unfortunately—whether left- or right-wing—subjugation ends predictably: an arrogant, power-hungry elite manipulating populations to enrich themselves.

Again, imperialists conquer with armies; Marxists conquer with ideas. Instead of subjugating by force, Marxism persuades the young and inexperienced that the freedoms of Western culture should be replaced with the government control of socialism.[37]

For generations, we have been taught to accept—without question—that *government* is the solution to any problem. Are the same institutions that thrive on government power and corruption also propagating these narratives? Of course they are.

Imagine how different America would be if, instead, we had been taught—with equal intensity—that consumers already hold the power to keep industries and institutions in line.

The simple visual formulas in this program promote this understanding—and much more: the ability to see through divisive propaganda, resist corruption, and better defend freedom in everyday life.

From the Author:

When I first noticed the corruption in our institutions, I thought I could simply alert others, and they would be just as outraged as I was. Instead, as I mentioned earlier, I was disturbed to find that many otherwise intelligent people were—and still are—willing to hate friends and family based on fact-free name-calling from well-coiffed strangers in a box on their wall. This is one of the reasons—like so many others—I "left the Left."[38]

I would show these people hard evidence—statistics, videos, even in-your-face common sense—and their eyes just glaze over and they flee the discussion. For many, the idea that the nice people in those fancy "news" studios could be lying to them is simply too much to bear.

For a time, I thought that, when push came to shove, these people would not prove to be as hateful as they seem. I was wrong. The reaction to Charlie Kirk's death shook many of us to the core.[39] Ironically—far from the villain the media portrayed—Charlie Kirk was a peaceful man of genuine kindness whose only "crime" was debating in defense of heartfelt Christian values.[40]

Without knowing a single thing about Mr. Kirk's actual views—and many never having even *heard of him*—countless leftists accepted the lie that he was a "hateful racist" and they publicly rejoiced at his death.[41] Sadly, this was not just a fanatical few.

Many in today's left, convinced by corrupt media of their "moral superiority," literally believe that the murder of Christian conservatives—*good people*—should be condoned and even celebrated.

I used to wonder how Germans could be manipulated into hating Jews so deeply[42] that they condoned systematic murder, or how Chinese students could be talked into publicly humiliating innocent teachers, landlords, and business owners during "struggle sessions."[43]

Now I know. This is where evil lives—in the weak-minded, for whom group consensus outweighs truth and human decency.

And here's the kicker: Under the influence of neo-Marxism, nearly every narrative that so-called "liberals" support today is engineered to be destructive. This is illustrated in Formula 2A, page 38. So they literally cheered for the death of a good man because he refused to defend their toxic ideas.

This kind of blind obedience to harmful doctrine does not happen by accident; it is the product of long-term psychological conditioning.

Yuri Bezmenov, a former KGB officer turned defector, offered valuable insights into Soviet psychological-warfare tactics and their application to the U.S. population. His interviews and lectures from the 1980s remain shockingly relevant.[44] An excerpt from one of his interviews is on the facing page.

Adults who still support the left today are likely too far gone to even consider they might be wrong. That's why this program is designed to teach critical thinking *before* indoctrination takes hold.

Though we are late to the battle, we hold the advantage: truth is mightier than lies, and good is eminently more defensible than evil.

"The demoralization process in the United States is basically completed already. For the last 25 [or 35] years—actually, it's over-fulfilled—because demoralization now reaches such areas where previously not even Comrade Andropov and all his experts would have even dreamed of such tremendous success. Most of it is being done by Americans to Americans, thanks to a lack of moral standards.

As I mentioned before, exposure to true information does not matter anymore. A person who is demoralized is unable to assess true information. The facts tell nothing to him. Even if I shower him with information, with authentic proof, with documents, with pictures. Even if I take him by force to the Soviet Union and show him a concentration camp, he will refuse to believe it—until he is going to receive a kick in his fat bottom. When the military boot crushes his [expletive], then he will understand—but not before that. That is the tragedy of the situation of demoralization."[45]

—Yuri Bezmenov, interviewed by G. Edward Griffin, 1984

Yuri Bezmenov
Former KGB turned defector

DEMARXIFICATION—PAGE 8

For too long, Marxists have dominated academia with little to no opposition.

It's time we entered the fray…

Welcome to the formulas…

Section 1

FORMULA 1A
Appreciating Freedom, Rejecting Corruption

FORMULA 1B
The False Narrative of the "Oppressed" vs. the "Oppressor"

FORMULA 1C
Levels of Corruption

FORMULA 1A

Appreciating Freedom, Rejecting Corruption

Generations of Americans have grown up without a clear understanding of why freedom is our greatest treasure or how corruption is our greatest foe. Today, students are misled into believing that capitalism—economic freedom—is "evil," and that socialism—government subjugation—is "compassionate." This formula, used in discussion and debate, clarifies that freedom is indeed not slavery.[46] Corruption is the enemy. Socialism is sneaky imperialism—and much more.

We can plot anything—individuals, ideas, institutions, industries—on the formula below.

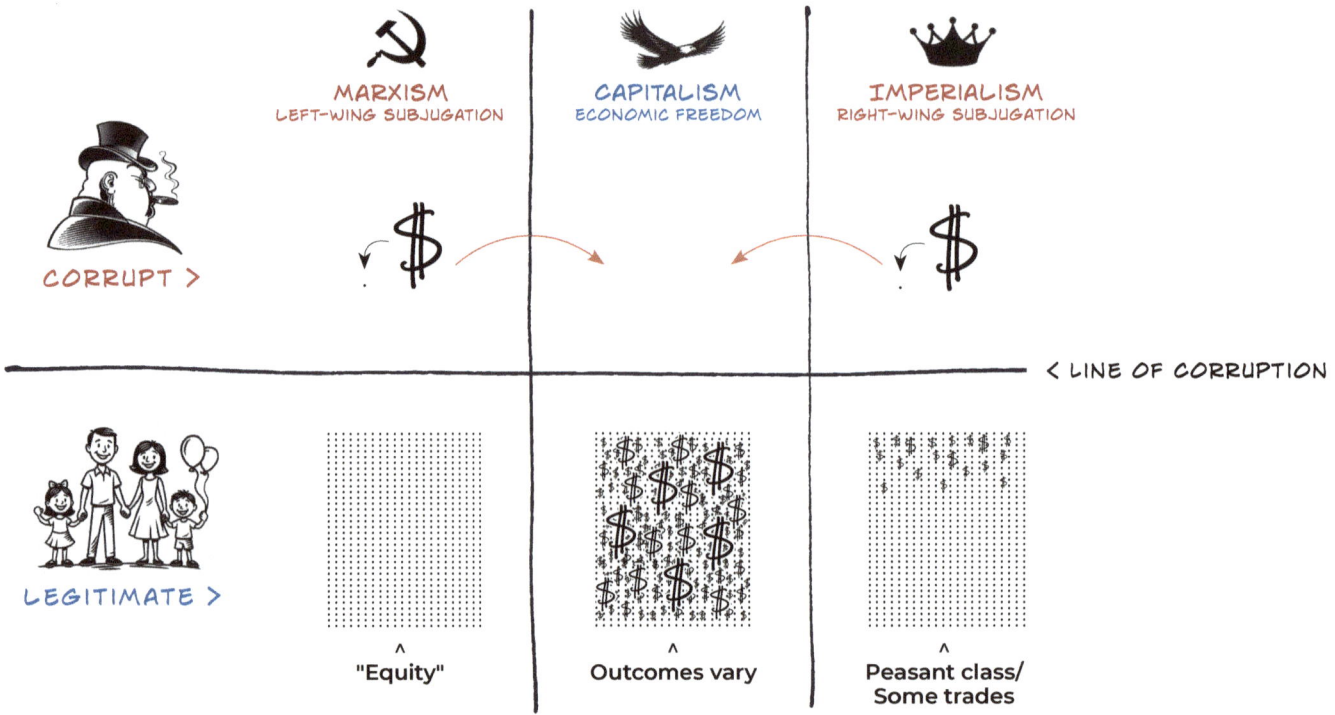

IMPORTANT TERMINOLOGY DEFINITIONS:

As noted previously, Karl Marx himself popularized the negative-sounding term *capitalism* as the word used to describe economic freedom. Over time, major dictionaries have diluted its definition, with Merriam-Webster now the only one still including the word *free*. This ambiguity is not harmless—the absence of a clear term for economic freedom undermines our ability to understand and achieve it.

In this program, we use the definition taught in 1970s grade schools: *Capitalism: the free exchange of goods and services* —meaning a competitive, free-market system in which private entities *voluntarily* exchange goods and services.

When people are forced or deceived into transactions, we will refer to that as either *imperialism* or *Marxism*.

We will use the term imperialism as an umbrella term for right-wing subjugation because it has historically been used in discourse alongside capitalism and Marxism.[47] Additional terms for each are on page 14.

The terms *Marxism*, *communism*, and *socialism* will be used to refer to left-wing subjugation.

At the top of the formula we plot CORRUPT individuals who throughout history, and today, instigate conflict, misery, and exploitation. They rarely fight in the wars they create and are seldom held accountable for their actions. Not all leaders belong above the LINE OF CORRUPTION, but sadly today it is essential to teach young people to identify those who are engaging in CORRUPTION and those who are not...

At the bottom of the formula we place LEGITIMATE populations who seek only a good life for their families. These populations suffer at the hands of the CORRUPT. They are conditioned—or forced—to fight wars they didn't start and finance the lifestyle and ambitions of the corrupt individuals at the top.

We all should be able to agree: we want the best for LEGITIMATE people, and the CORRUPT should be disempowered. More about this on page 17.

IMPERIALISM The right-hand column in the formula on the facing page illustrates conditions for most of history: **right-wing subjugation.** From one person owning a single slave to kings, emperors, warlords, caliphs, and fascist regimes, all of these dictatorships belong in the imperialist column. Although some individuals within the subjugated engage in trade, most of these populations are peasants.

CAPITALISM The middle column represents an *ideal*—a visualization of a *purely* capitalist, **or economically free**, society with *zero* corruption, where legitimate populations enjoy various outcomes based on competition, merit, innovation, and hard work. Unfortunately, this ideal has not existed on any large scale. Even in mostly capitalist nations, such as the United States, MARXISM and IMPERIALISM corrupt the economy and culture. This is represented by the red arrows left and right.

MARXISM The left-hand column depicts **left-wing subjugation**, the Marxist ideal—**communism.** The identical dots symbolize its unreachable goal of "equity": the belief that everyone should have the same outcome in life. **Socialism**, defined as government ownership or control of the means of production, is known as the pathway to that ideal. But seizing the means of production and enforcing uniformity requires submission of far too much power to a centralized authority. In practice, these authorities live like kings while populations starve, are executed, or imprisoned, and are sometimes desperate enough to engage in cannibalism.[48] Marxism poses as the alternative to imperialism but is simply *imperialism in disguise*. Marxism's recurring patterns are revealed in Formulas 1B and 2A.

CORRUPT >

LEGITIMATE >

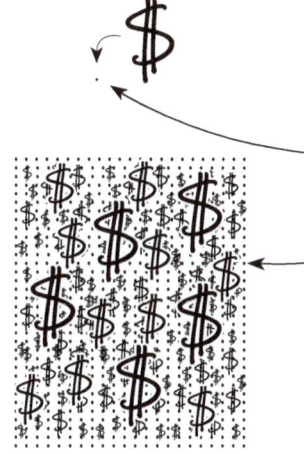

Centralization Ensures Corruption

Mathematically, it's easier to corrupt centralized authorities—represented by this dot—than it is to corrupt an entire population represented by these dollar signs (businesses) and dots (workers).

Corrupting a single entity can be done with money, power, blackmail, or manipulation.[49] Corrupting an entire population is more difficult. One solution to disempower the corrupt is explored in Formula 2C.

DEMARXIFICATION.COM—PAGE 13

Throughout this program, we will use "CAPITALISM," "IMPERIALISM," and "MARXISM" as blanket terms, including but not limited to the lists of terms beneath each:

MARXISM
LEFT-WING SUBJUGATION

Classism
Collectivism
Communism
Gramscianism
Leninism
Maoism
Marxism
Marxism-Leninism
Neo-Marxism
Nihilism
Post-modernism
Proletarianism
Relativism
Socialism
Stalinism
Subjectivism
Trotskyism
Wokeism

CAPITALISM
ECONOMIC FREEDOM

Anarchy†
Capitalism†
Democracy‡
Emancipation‡
Freedom
Independence‡
Individualism
Liberty‡
Populism†
Republic‡

IMPERIALISM
RIGHT-WING SUBJUGATION

Aristocracy*
Authoritarianism
Autocracy
Absolutism
Caliphate
Colonialism*
Caste
Cronyism
Czarism*
Despotism
Dictatorship*
Domination
Enslavement
Exploitation
Fascism
Feudalism*
Hegemony
Imperialism*
Monarchy*
Monocracy
Monopoly*
Nazism
Oligarchy*
Oppression
Repression
Royalty*
Serfdom*
Slavery
Subjugation
Suppression
Technocracy*
Theocracy*
Totalitarianism
Tyranny

† Terms for freedom that have acquired negative connotations or are being reframed negatively.

‡ Terms for freedom with alternate definitions, such as those describing both "the state of being free" and "freedom *from*" something; or terms that involve "representatives."

* Terms for right-wing exploitation that are not inherently malevolent—e.g., a "benevolent dictatorship." These can be evaluated on a case-by-case basis.

The inclusion or exclusion of specific terms can be subject for discussion.

If you want to change the definition of capitalism so that it can mean both *freedom* and *slavery*, then it becomes a contranym and effectively meaningless.

We have plenty of words for exploitation.
Why so few that mean the pure state of freedom?

ERASING THE IDEA OF FREEDOM...

Marxists' objective is to remove the terminology for economic freedom from the equation altogether.

MARXISM
LEFT-WING SUBJUGATION

CAPITALISM
ECONOMIC FREEDOM

IMPERIALISM
RIGHT-WING SUBJUGATION

"In North Korea, there is no word for love. There is no word for human rights. There's no word for liberty. Dictators removed the word from our dictionary. Because you know what? If you don't know the word, that means you don't know the concept. That's how they control your thinking, your thoughts."

—*Yeonmi Park, American author, human-rights activist & North Korean defector*[50]

Today, throughout American institutions, the economic freedom of capitalism is consistently conflated with the exploitation of slavery. These are not merely different, but polar opposites...

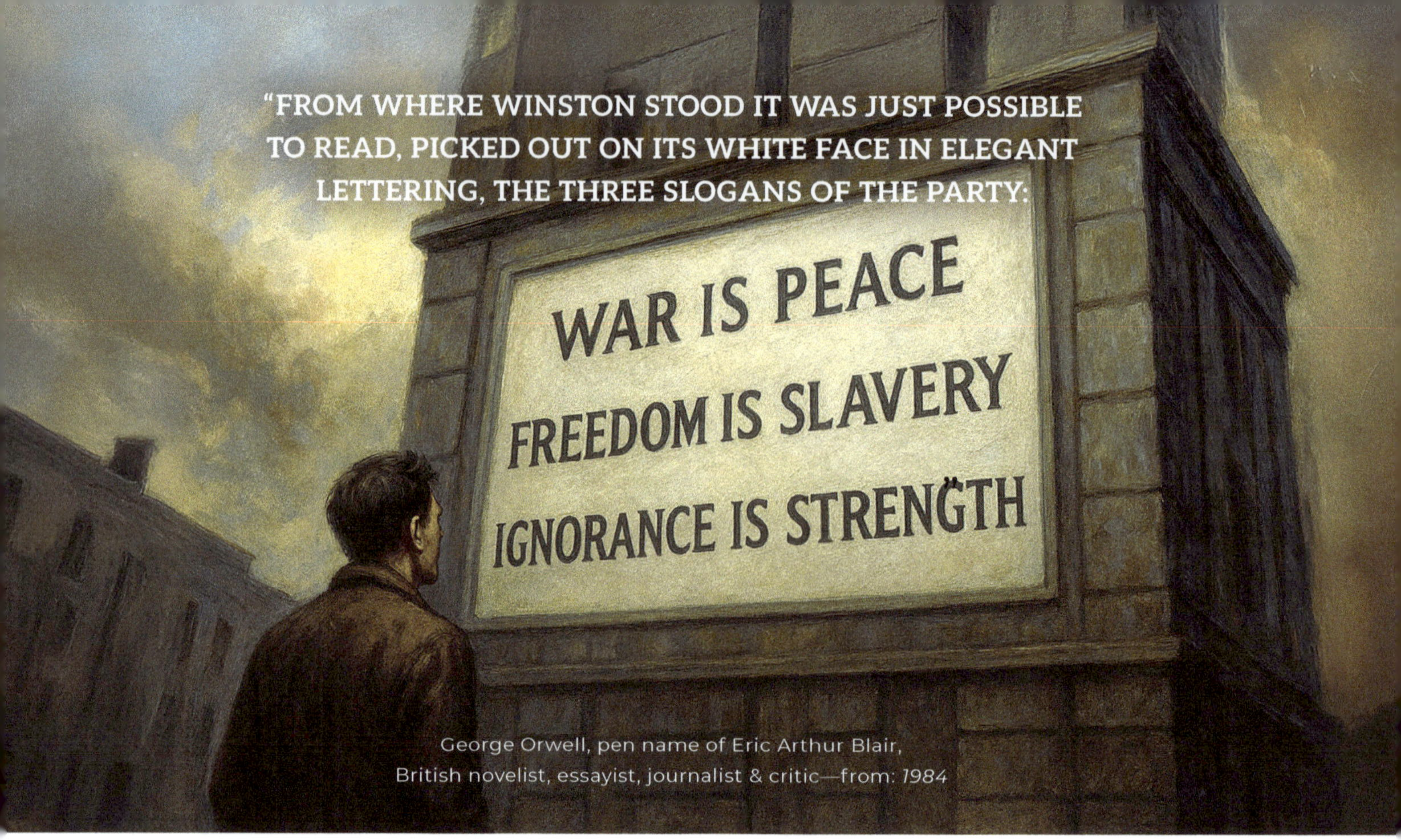

> "FROM WHERE WINSTON STOOD IT WAS JUST POSSIBLE TO READ, PICKED OUT ON ITS WHITE FACE IN ELEGANT LETTERING, THE THREE SLOGANS OF THE PARTY:
>
> WAR IS PEACE
> FREEDOM IS SLAVERY
> IGNORANCE IS STRENGTH

George Orwell, pen name of Eric Arthur Blair, British novelist, essayist, journalist & critic—from: *1984*

ONE TOXIC DECEPTION OF MARXISM: "FREEDOM IS SLAVERY."

In true Orwellian fashion, generations of Americans are being misled to believe that "freedom is slavery."

Books such as Howard Zinn's *A People's History of the United States*[51] and the New York Times' *The 1619 Project: A New Origin Story*[52] mislabel historic actions as *capitalism*, which should properly be defined as *imperialism*—and were often carried out by *literal* imperialists. They also omit history based on actual capitalism (economic freedom) on which the U.S. achieved the level of success we enjoy today.

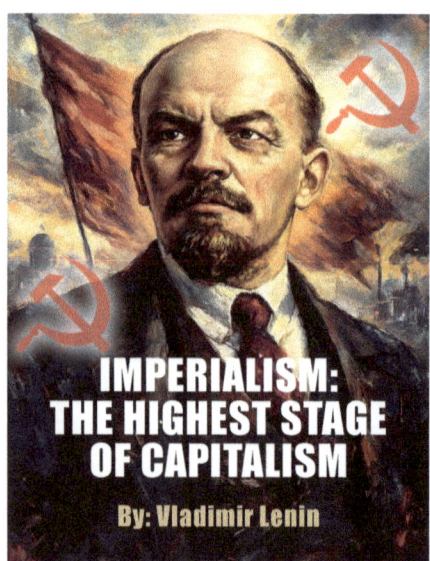

Whether it is the above authors' intention or not, confusing capitalism with imperialism reflects a Marxist tactic reminiscent of communist dictators like Vladimir Lenin, whose work *Imperialism: The Highest Stage of Capitalism*[53] illustrates this deception.

The recent "No Kings" protests reek of communist influence. The slogan itself is not something Americans would say—it sounds more like a literal translation from Chinese. Straight out of the communist playbook, it paints a blatantly *capitalist* president as an *imperialist*.

It is imperative that we begin to teach—as illustrated in Formula 1A—that Marxism (communism and socialism) is actually the highest stage of imperialism, and that capitalism (economic freedom) is the polar opposite of both.

How to debate—and find agreement with—a socialist using Formula 1A:

Question: "What is the basic goal you believe socialism will achieve?"
Presumably, they hope to achieve…

…the best outcomes for LEGITIMATE families regardless of economic or social status, and…

…freedom from CORRUPTION and exploitation by those with excessive money and power.

On the above, we all agree—but regarding how to achieve this, we strongly disagree…

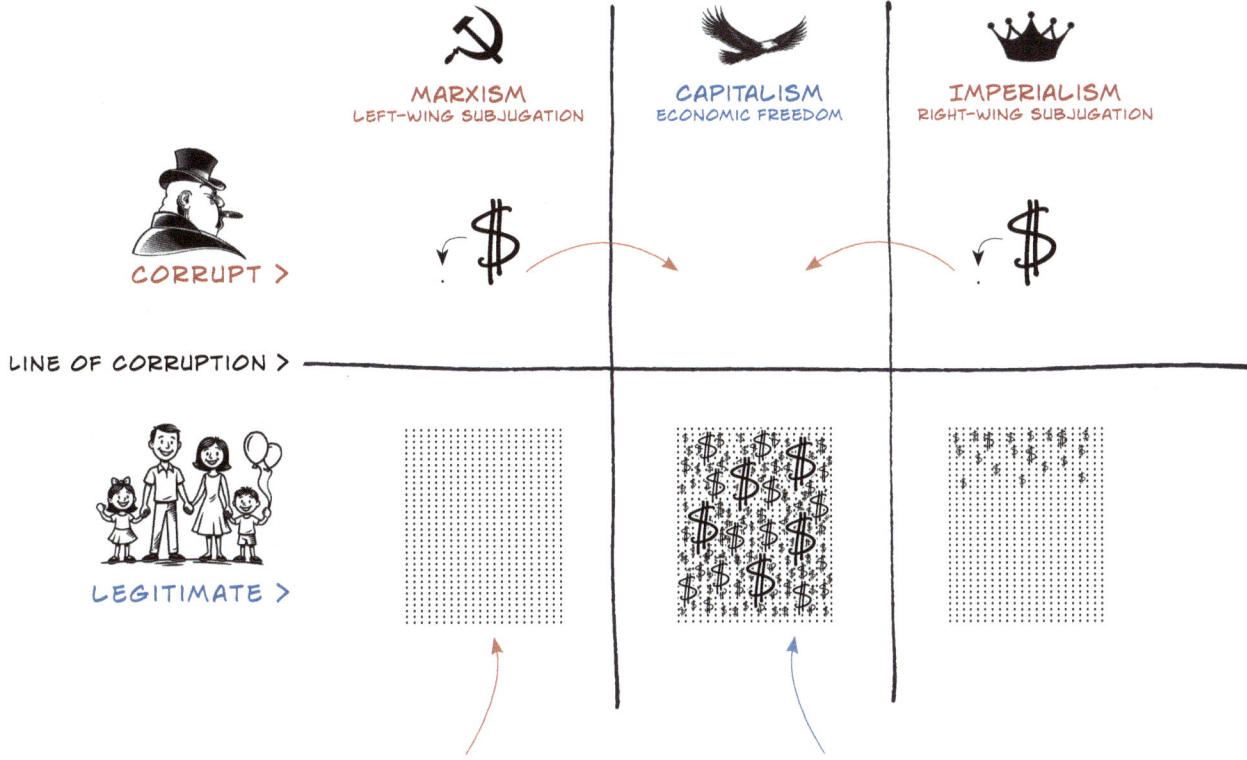

MARXISTS mislead inexperienced young people into believing that the equity depicted here is fair and desirable—and that government should be empowered to enforce it.

What could go wrong there?

In true Marxist fashion, "socialism" promises power to the workers, but delivers the opposite. Empowering government to seize private businesses strips workers of choice, leverage, and the opportunity to become entrepreneurs..

The socialist answer to owners doing better than workers? A centralized authority assuring no one does well—except, of course, for themselves and their cronies.[54]

Socialism is IMPERIALISM with better branding.

The CAPITALIST solution? Legit entrepreneurs and consumers exercise the power we've had all along.

We outnumber the corrupt by vast amounts—and we generate and circulate the very money they need to survive.

Government should also be reimagined so that agencies are subject to free market competition *wherever possible*.

This is explored in Formula 3C, page 62.

On the x-axis of Formula 1A, we divide exploitation into Marxism and Imperialism based on the means by which each spearheads their efforts to enslave and exploit free people.

Of course, both employ all methods of putting free people under authoritarian control, such as taxation, regulation, and often by force.

The distinction below is helpful in recognizing that Marxism is not an "alternative" to imperialism. It's simply a deceptive means to achieve domination of populations who would recognize and reject blatant Imperialism and other forms of overt tyranny...

MARXISM VS. IMPERIALISM

Marxism	Imperialism
Achieve power through breadlines	Achieve power through bloodlines
Harm by "giving"[55]	Harm by taking
Generally claim to be "for the worker"	Generally claim to be "for the country"
Infiltrate colleges and institutions to break moral compasses and divide populations	Roll in with tanks, guns, or authoritarian dictates backed up by force
Tend to use covert methods	Tend to use overt methods
Tend to invade from within	Tend to invade from outside
Implement taxation allegedly for the "oppressed"	Implement taxation allegedly for "defense" or "your safety"
Will generally demonize groups within a population	Will generally demonize foreign leaders & populations
Psychological warfare	Physical warfare
Institutional & economic domination	Military & economic domination
Populations tend to be unaware of the threat	Populations tend to be aware of the threat
Take over can happen over generations	Take over can happen relatively quickly
Colonization through "migration"	Blatant colonization
Openly desire to tear down society	Openly desire to enrich themselves
Claims moral superiority	Claims national superiority

Often, countries jump out of the frying pan (imperialism) and into the fire (communism or socialism). For example, following the Bolshevik Revolution, Russia transitioned from imperialism to communism in a short period of time, almost completely bypassing the economic freedom of capitalism altogether.[56]

Capitalism and the United States are falsely demeaned, and populations are misled into believing that Marxism is "the answer." In reality, Marxism is nothing but sneaky imperialism, and capitalism (economic freedom) is the antidote to both...

As mentioned earlier, ideal capitalism has not existed on any large scale. But, it is crucial that we work toward achieving it. Here are just some ideals we could be working toward.

CAPITALISM (IDEAL)

A limited government exists to determine and implement the will of the people, inform consumers, and arbitrate in cases of harm to others.

Encourage strong families & healthy communities

Legitimate economic competition

Business is regulated by consumers, not by centralized authorities

Encourage small, local business & private contractors

"Taxpayer Choice" voucher systems for collective needs

Defensive-only military

Free trade with free countries

Promote freedom in other countries

Marxists have done a tremendous job popularizing socialism and demonizing capitalism. It is long past time to begin teaching students to consider how to achieve the above ideals of freedom instead of the socialist subjugation they are being deceived into supporting.

On the following pages are examples related to the y-axis of Formula 1A.

EXAMPLE: LEGITIMATE VS. CORRUPT—A SMALL TOWN

LEGITIMATE Societies Build:

Let's take an early 20th-century American town where small businesses compete fairly and no one exploits others. People freely exchange goods and services at prices they willingly pay and accept.

One day, a large coal deposit is discovered nearby. Four mining companies move in, and the town doubles in size. At first, the companies compete legitimately—each striving to produce better coal, faster and cheaper, through innovation and sound business practices.

With four operations vying for workers, wages rise. Miners' families spend their earnings at local shops, which expand to carry additional goods, improving life for everyone. Prosperity lifts the banks too, allowing more lending. Businesses hire more people, including miners' families, who in turn spend more. The need for coal increases along with profits for the coal companies.

As the community thrives, charitable needs are met because families and successful businesses have money to give. Freedom and fair trade create an upward spiral of prosperity for all.

But such success is fragile...

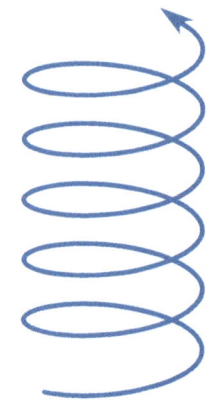

FREE MARKETS CREATE AN UPWARD SPIRAL

CORRUPT Monopolies Destroy:

After a time, in the aforementioned town, two of the mine owners sell out to the other two. The remaining two engage in corruption.

They believe it's a good idea to close two mines and lay off many miners. As a result—instead of mine owners competing for workers—workers are competing for jobs. They can exploit miners' desperation by lowering their wages.

At the same time, the corrupt mine owners believe they can exploit customers by raising the price of coal, because they no longer have competition.

The growth of the town has now reversed.

Coal miners are out of work or making less money, so their families are spending less. Small businesses suffer from the impoverishment of their customer base. They can no longer pay employees or make payments on loans. Businesses and banks fail, causing a downward spiral for the entire community.

Ironically, the corrupt individuals are not only harming the community, they are harming *themselves*. When a community is impoverished, they have less money to purchase coal, so they look for alternatives. In addition, disgruntled workers may not work as hard as happy workers with financial motivation.

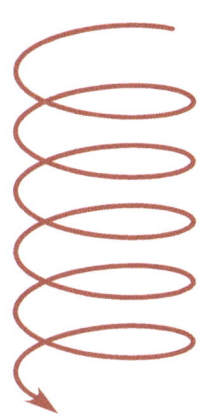

CORRUPTION CREATES A DOWNWARD SPIRAL

SOLUTIONS:

Please note that I used the example of an "early American" town because, in a society based on economic freedom, communities have options for dealing with corruption, monopolies, and exploitation.

In a free country, other business owners would not necessarily have ties to the coal-mine owners. Also harmed by their corruption, these owners—along with the rest of the townspeople—could take any number of actions against them. Collective boycotts, strikes, protests, and negotiations could be employed.

Early Americans could shun and refuse to do business with individuals who were harming the community.

In contrast, in a country under imperial rule—such as pre-industrial European communities—imperial elites close ranks against rebellion. This makes it far more difficult, if not impossible, for a population to overcome corruption.

As mentioned in the introduction, it was the creation of employment options through capitalism that ended the reign of imperialists. Where Marxism was implemented, far worse subjugation followed.

EXAMPLE: AMERICAN PHARMACEUTICAL CORRUPTION

Americans foot the bill for pharmaceutical profits—first through taxes that fund Big Pharma's research, then at the insurance exchange, and again at the pharmacy counter. In addition, those same companies enjoy legal protection from Congress under legislation such as the deceptively named *National Childhood Vaccine Injury Act of 1986*,[62] which shields Big Pharma from accountability when their products cause harm or death.

American healthcare is by far the most expensive[57] yet is dead last among wealthy nations in life expectancy, infant and maternal health, and preventable deaths.[58] I have heard the claim that this is due to our "capitalist" healthcare system, but...

...today's American healthcare system is <u>not</u> capitalist...

Medicare and Medicaid are government-run, centrally managed programs—socialist in structure and funding.

Obamacare delivers the worst of both worlds: a government-run marketplace offering only a handful of private mega-insurers in each state. These insurers aligned with government, resulting in limited competition and a marketplace where prices are essentially fixed.

American doctors must follow protocols set by centralized institutions which are heavily influenced by insurance and pharmaceutical interests such as the FDA. Diet and exercise are given little consideration in medical schools[59]—or in treatment—in favor of more lucrative pharmaceuticals and surgeries.[60] Doctors who deviate jeopardize their ability to accept insurance and can even lose their licenses.

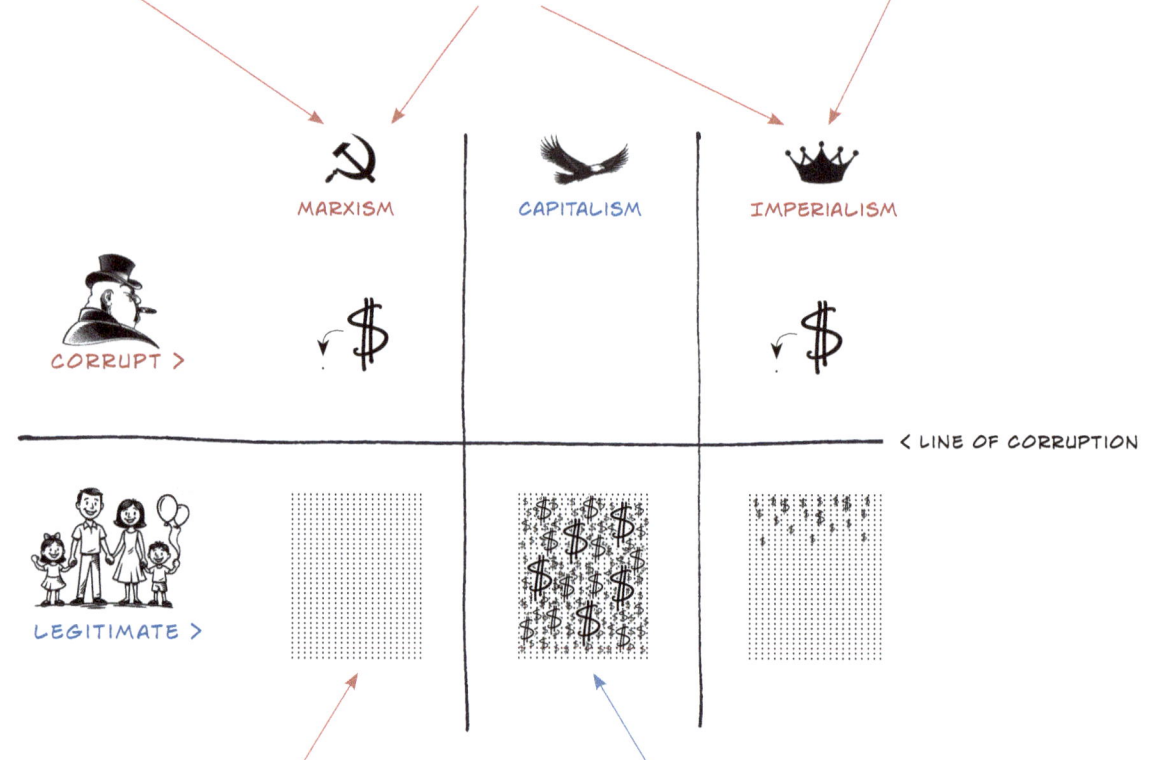

Many individuals have been misled into believing that "public" healthcare is the answer. But "public" means government-run, which all but assures apathy (think DMV), incompetence, waste, and often corruption—because authorities face no competition.

Real solutions include Health Savings Accounts (HSAs)[61] or voucher systems—*operating within free markets*. When providers are not held hostage by self-serving institutions, consumers regain power, and providers are free to explore treatments based on patient outcomes rather than on profit margins.

The concept of vouchers is explored on page 62.

EXAMPLE: AMERICAN ACADEMIC CORRUPTION

American college students are immersed in anti-freedom and anti-American narratives, eliminating their motivation to defend our nation, its borders, and its liberties. Despite being known as a beacon of freedom—and one of the *least racist* nations—colleges and other institutions teach the opposite, labeling anything associated with—or in support of—the U.S. as "racist."

The level of demonization applied to a particular target is likely proportionate to its enemies' desire to destroy it. The U.S. must be target number one...

United States—"racist"
Americans—"racist"
Capitalism—"racist"
Patriotism—"racist"
Prayer—"racist"
Borders—"racist"
American flag—"racist"
White people—"racist"
National anthem—"racist"
Founding fathers—"racist"
U.S. Constitution—"racist"
Betsy Ross—"racist"
Western culture—"racist"
Traditional family—"racist"
Hard work—"racist"
Punctuality—"racist"
Facts—"racist"
Statistics—"racist"
Republicans—"racist"
Conservatives—"racist"
Classical literature—"racist"
Fine art—"racist"
Classical music—"racist"
Ballet—"racist"
Shakespeare—"racist"
Law enforcement—"racist"
Border security—"racist"

ICE—"racist"
Black Friday—"racist"
Black holes—"racist"
Math—"racist"
Grades—"racist"
Proper English—"racist"
Diet & exercise—"racist"
Palm trees—"racist"
Milk—"racist"
Cauliflower—"racist"
Eggplant—"racist"
Syrup—"racist"
Ice cream trucks—"racist"
Halloween—"racist"
Christmas—"racist"
Santa—"racist"
Peanut butter & jelly—"racist"
Doing well in school—"racist"
Black conservatives—"racist"
Gay conservatives—"racist"
Hispanic conservatives—"racist"
Stepping aside when a person of color is walking toward you—"racist"
Not stepping aside when a person of color is walking toward you—"racist"
Etc.

Here too, what are the odds that the thorough demonization above is naturally occurring and not the result of intentional psychological warfare against the United States and Western culture?

Why do so many people from diverse cultures flee to the U.S. if America is so "racist?"

It is sad that so many have been convinced to disdain the nation that has done so much good for so many people. Ironically, claiming that values such as hard work and punctuality are "racist" or characteristics of "whiteness"—in true Marxist fashion—is itself racist and insulting to people of color, as illustrated by the hideous poster[63] produced by the *Smithsonian National Museum of African American History & Culture*.

Formula 1B, page 26, illustrates the Marxist "oppressed vs. oppressor" narrative—the impetus for the name-calling above.

Following, we examine the x-axis of Formula 1A: important distinctions between imperialism, capitalism, and Marxism...

EXAMPLE: MARXISM, CAPITALISM & IMPERIALISM—A FARMER'S MARKET

For decades, a seasoned farmer has been growing and selling carrots at the village market. Despite their mediocre quality, the townsfolk have grown accustomed to them, given the absence of competition in the carrot-growing domain.

However, the status quo shifts when a fresh face emerges in the farming community. Recognizing the sub-par quality of the incumbent farmer's carrots, she decides to enter the market. Venturing to the general store, she peruses catalogs and selects new types of carrot seeds. Implementing innovative cultivation and harvesting methods, she offers a variety of carrots for a better price.

Before long, her carrots captivate the market, drawing customers from the established farmer to her new enterprise. Her actions are those of a free-market CAPITALIST.

Below, we offer accounts of how the original carrot farmer responds under each ideology...

MARXIST:

Marxism didn't exist in this era, but if it had, the new farmer would have no impetus to compete in the first place. But let's say an emerging Marxist society, the original farmer would falsely brand his rival "racist" and her customers as "bad people." Through social pressure, he turns the community against her until she's driven out of business.

Everyone loses. She faces ruin, her employees and their families struggle, new carrots are no longer available, and bitterness divides the town.

CAPITALIST:

Adopting a free-market capitalist mindset, the farmer innovates—visiting the general store, browsing seed catalogs, and ordering new vegetable varieties. Instead of carrots, he rotates his crops, and begins growing specialty produce for the local community.

In this scenario, both farmers prosper, the community enjoys a wider selection of vegetables for their families, and animosity is replaced by healthy competition.

IMPERIALIST:

Without having been taught the value of innovation, the original carrot farmer instead incites his workers, blaming the newcomer for losses. He leads them to her farm stand with torches and pitchforks; she's driven out of business.

But this aggression also leads to loss for all. The ousted farmer and her workers suffer, the town loses produce variety and jobs, and although his carrots sell again, they are bought out of fear, not freedom. He is resented by all.

Again, legitimate competition enriches all—domination harms all, even the dominators.

USING FORMULA 1A TO DEFEND FREEDOM (CAPITALISM):

Once an individual becomes familiar with Formula 1A, they will not forget that slavery, stolen land, sweatshop labor, and other forms of exploitation belong in the *imperialism* column—not the *capitalism* column…

1 When a company engages in corrupt practices with an African dictator to exploit African peoples and seize their natural resources, it is often mislabeled as "capitalism." It isn't. It's imperialism. Capitalism—economic freedom—is what African populations actually need.[64]

2 Are the high crime rates and pervasiveness of drug addiction in impoverished neighborhoods the result of capitalism? Or, is the issue actually the *absence* of capitalism due to the U.S. welfare system (socialist-based exploitation) and drug cartels (imperialist-based exploitation) in these communities?

3 Venezuelan populations were essentially capitalist during the 1950s to the early 1980s, a period characterized by high oil revenues, economic growth, and the highest standard of living in Latin America.

4 Today, they are victims of both the oppression of a socialist government and the imperialist tyranny of drug cartels.

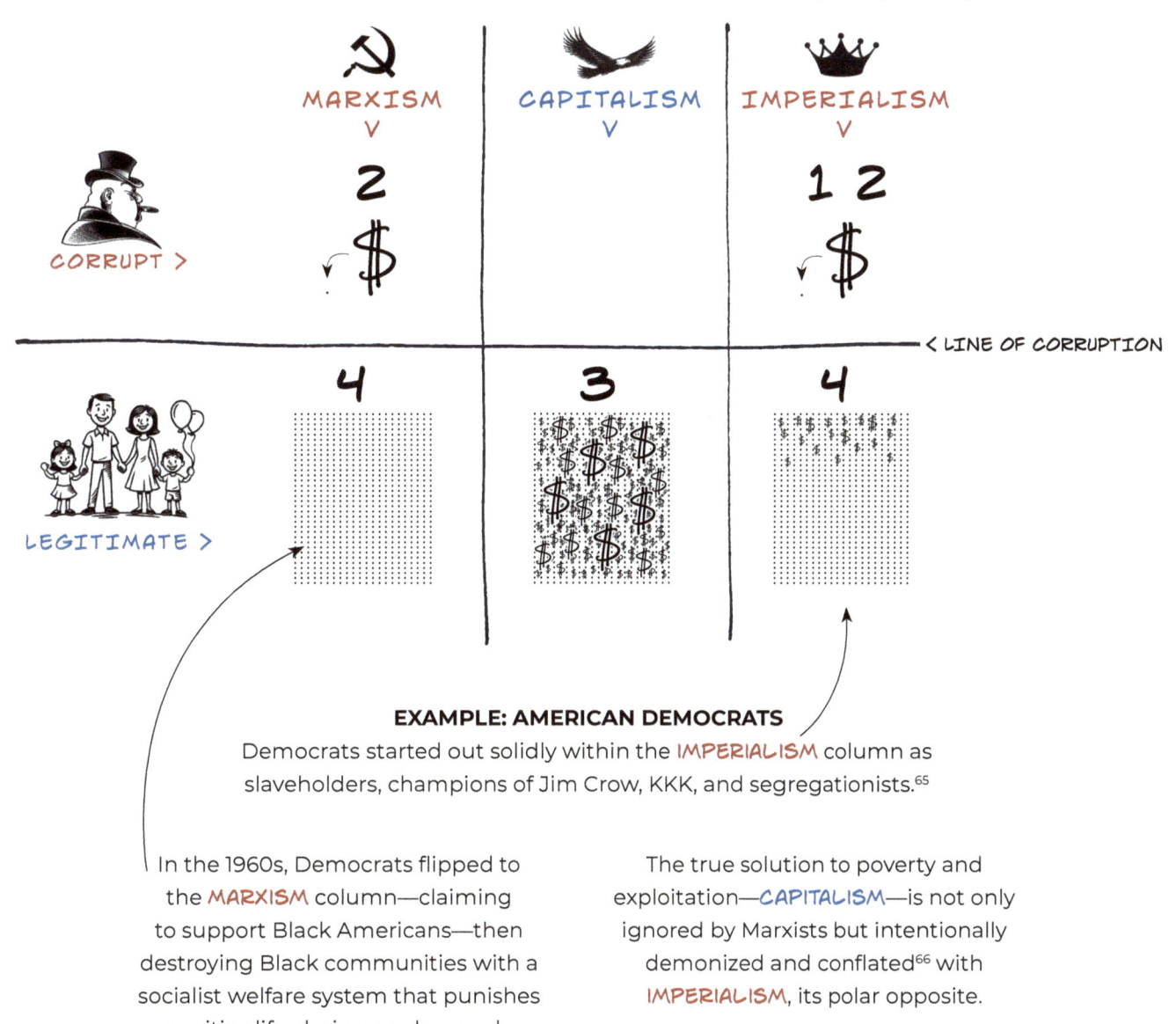

EXAMPLE: AMERICAN DEMOCRATS
Democrats started out solidly within the IMPERIALISM column as slaveholders, champions of Jim Crow, KKK, and segregationists.[65]

In the 1960s, Democrats flipped to the MARXISM column—claiming to support Black Americans—then destroying Black communities with a socialist welfare system that punishes positive life choices and rewards negative ones. (More on page 68.)

The true solution to poverty and exploitation—CAPITALISM—is not only ignored by Marxists but intentionally demonized and conflated[66] with IMPERIALISM, its polar opposite.

FORMULA 1B

The False Narrative of the "Oppressed" vs. the "Oppressor"

In *The Communist Manifesto,* Marx framed history as a struggle between "oppressors" and "oppressed." Following this formula, today's leftist institutions have divided Western societies.

The oppression may be real, exaggerated, historical, or completely fabricated.

When people of different backgrounds work or socialize together, friendship comes naturally—but powerful interests know that divided populations are easier to control.

The true enemy is not our neighbor but those who manufacture division. The more we're pitted against one another, the less we notice *their* corruption.

This formula enables students to recognize and reject individuals and institutions that advance the "oppressed vs. oppressor" narratives.

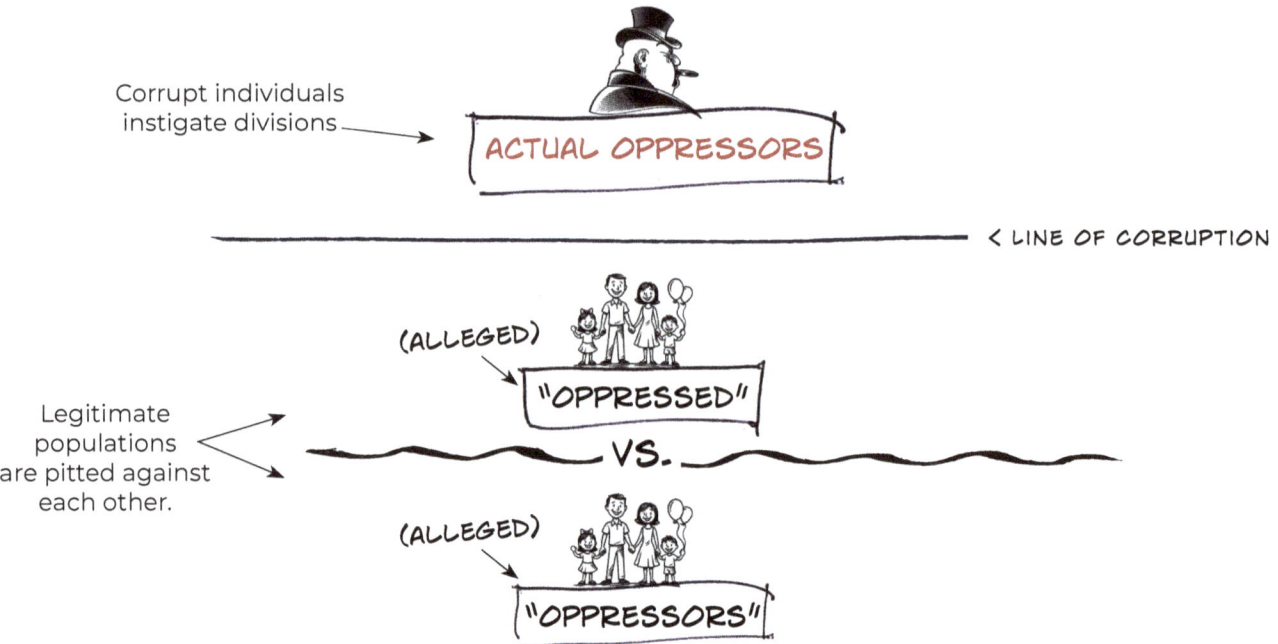

History shows repeated examples of regimes dividing their own populations into hostile groups.

In the Soviet Union, so-called "Kulaks" were pitted against everyone else; in Rwanda, Tutsis and Hutus were set against each other; and in Communist China, "Black Chinese" were vilified in contrast to "Red Chinese."

In these and many other cases, both groups were devastated by such divisions, while the true oppressors—corrupt authorities who orchestrate the conflicts—are seldom identified as the instigators or held accountable for the divisions.[67]

TRIPLE STANDARDS:

We are all familiar with the term "double standards." In this *false* narrative of the "oppressed" and the "oppressor," we have "triple standards."

STANDARDS FOR THE CORRUPT, THE
ACTUAL OPPRESSORS

As stated earlier, throughout history these individuals have fueled war, spread injustice, and caused untold death and suffering. They sow division among ordinary people and are the *true oppressors*.

Because they control narratives and legal systems, they usually escape justice and moral accountability. They are rarely held to the standards they impose on everyone else.

─────────────────────────── < LINE OF CORRUPTION

STANDARDS FOR THE ALLEGED "OPPRESSORS"	STANDARDS FOR THE ALLEGED "OPPRESSED"
Labeled as "oppressors," "privileged," etc. →	Labeled as "oppressed," "victims," etc.
Are not permitted to have gatherings or clubs →	Are permitted to have gatherings and clubs
Are taught to be ashamed →	Are allowed to be proud
Can be judged and characterized as a group →	Must not be judged or characterized as a group
"Diversity" is allegedly a strength for these groups →	Desire for ethnic purity is acceptable for these groups
Must follow speech codes →	Can speak freely
Are generally held legally and criminally responsible for their own actions →	Are *also* generally held legally and criminally responsible for their own actions
Are held morally responsible for their own actions →	Are *not* held morally responsible for their own actions
Are held morally responsible for the actions of: their group, their ancestors, the "oppressed," and the actual oppressors →	Are rightfully not held morally responsible for the actions of their group, their ancestors, the "oppressors" or the actual oppressors

The vast majority of individuals within a group labeled as "oppressors" are blameless, never having participated in any form of oppression. Yet, they are targeted for demonization and blame by the actual oppressors—corrupt individuals in power.

Those labeled as "oppressed" may be oppressed—but *not necessarily*. Many powerful elites—*actual oppressors*—occupy the "oppressed" column by claiming victimhood based on their gender, sexuality, or ethnicity. Others, like leftists, occupy this column by claiming to *empathize* with the "oppressed."

EXAMPLE: UNITED STATES TODAY

As mentioned earlier, "ideal" capitalism—economic freedom with zero corruption—has not been achieved on any large scale.

As illustrated *above the line of corruption*, the United States has a *mixed* economy: generally CAPITALIST, but influenced by corruption from both the MARXIST left and the IMPERIALIST right, as illustrated below.

For instance, the U.S. welfare system reflects MARXIST-BASED CORRUPTION, while unjust wars represent IMPERIALIST-BASED CORRUPTION.

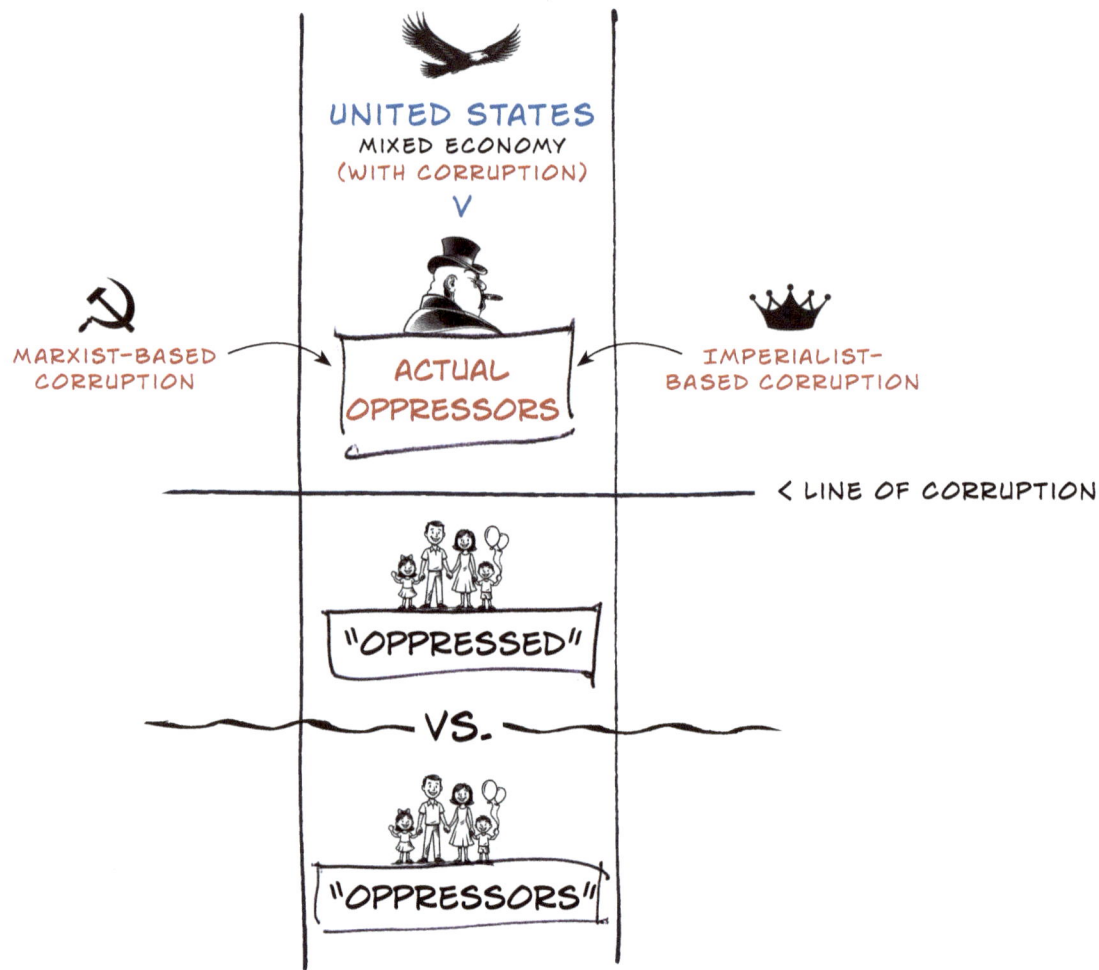

In the United States today, we face not just Marx's original class struggle—the proletariat (workers) vs. bourgeoisie (business owners)—but a relentless campaign by ACTUAL OPPRESSORS to pit nearly every demographic group into either the alleged "OPPRESSED" or the alleged "OPPRESSOR" categories, as listed on the facing page.

"If a kingdom is divided against itself, that kingdom cannot stand.
If a house is divided against itself, that house cannot stand."—*Mark 3:24–25*

 **ACTUAL OPPRESSORS** are those who create and propagate the divisions below.

< LINE OF CORRUPTION

Again, the divisions below can be true, historic, or completely fabricated, but these are the divisions Americans are subject to today

GROUPS:

"OPPRESSED" vs. "OPPRESSORS"

"OPPRESSED"	vs.	"OPPRESSORS"
Proletariat (workers)	vs.	Bourgeoisie (business owners)
Blacks	vs.	Whites
Women	vs.	Men
LGBTs	vs.	Heterosexuals
Criminals	vs.	Law enforcement
Impoverished	vs.	Wealthy
Everyone else	vs.	Americans
Trans-women	vs.	Women
Average	vs.	Gifted
Girl Scouts	vs.	Boy Scouts
Drug cartels	vs.	Border patrol
Child traffickers	vs.	ICE
Mindless protesters	vs.	Independent journalists
Left	vs.	Right
Vaxxed	vs.	Unvaxxed
Squatters	vs.	Home owners
Younger gens	vs.	Boomers
Everyone else	vs.	Judeo/Christians
Pro-choice	vs.	Pro-life
The planet	vs.	Humans
Minorities	vs.	Majorities
Climate alarmists	vs.	Climate realists
Illegal migrants	vs.	Citizens

It is time to teach against this divisiveness. We can begin with the fact that the staggering number of divisions we are subject to confirms intentional manipulation.

Who is doing this to us and what can be done to peacefully disempower them?

CONDITIONS FOR GROUPS:

"OPPRESSED" vs. "OPPRESSORS"

"OPPRESSED"	vs.	"OPPRESSORS"
"Underprivileged"	vs.	"Privileged"
"Victims of hate"	vs.	"Haters"
"Victims of racism"	vs.	"Racist"
"Victims of sexism"	vs.	"Sexist"
"Victims of homophobia"	vs.	"Homophobic"
"Victims of Islamophobia"	vs.	"Islamophobic"
"Victims of transphobia"	vs.	"Transphobic"
"Victims of xenophobia"	vs.	"Xenophobic"
"Victims of white supremacy"	vs.	"White supremacist"
"Repressed"	vs.	"Repressive"
"Victims of unfairness"	vs.	"Unfair"
"Inclusive"	vs.	"Not inclusive"
"Cool"	vs.	"Uncool"
"Cultured"	vs.	"Uncultured"
"Modern"	vs.	"Old fashioned"
"Open"	vs.	"Prudish"
"Worldly"	vs.	"Naive"
"Sophisticated"	vs.	"Unsophisticated"
"Urban"	vs.	"Redneck"
"Educated"	vs.	"Uneducated"
"For the poor"	vs.	"For the wealthy"
"Good person"	vs.	"Bad person"
"Victims of bigotry"	vs.	"Bigoted"
"Morally superior"	vs.	"Immoral"
"Liberal"	vs.	"Far right"
"Helping"	vs.	"Harmful"
"Victims of Nazis"	vs.	"Nazi"
"Victims of fascism"	vs.	"Fascist"
"Victims of the 'patriarchy'"	vs.	"The 'patriarchy'"
"Victims of antisemitism"	vs.	"Antisemitic"
"Victims of Christian dogma"	vs.	"Christian" (as if this is bad)
"Victims of conservatives"	vs.	"Conservative" (as if this is bad)
"For the children"	vs.	"Want dead children"
"For the planet"	vs.	"Planet hater"
"Believes in 'science'"	vs.	"Science 'denier'"
"Encouraging tolerance"	vs.	"Encouraging violence"
Etc.		Etc.

DEMARXIFICATION.COM—PAGE 29

WHO ARE BEING SCAPEGOATED AS "OPPRESSORS" TODAY?

Do a simple search for any of these terms:
"Oppression Matrix," "Systems of Domination," "Hierarchy of Identities," "Web of Oppression," "Power Dynamics," "Social Inequity Framework," "Interlocking Systems of Oppression," "Intersectionality."

There are literally hundreds of hate-filled bigoted charts masquerading as "virtuous"—like this one below—posted by institutions including colleges, churches, women's organizations and even in some organizations for the disabled.

"MATRIX OF OPPRESSION"			
SOCIAL IDENTITY	PRIVILEGED	TARGETED	BIASES WITH POWER
RACE	White/Caucasian	Asian, Black, Latinx, Native/Indigenous	Racism
GENDER	Gender Conforming (Cisgender), Identify as Male or Female	Transgender, Gender Queer, Intersex, Gender Ambiguous, Agender	Transphobia/Trans* Oppression
SEXUAL ORIENTATION	Heterosexual	Lesbian, Gay, Queer, Questioning, Aces (Asexual/Aromantic), Polyamorous	Heterosexism, Homophobia
SOCIAL STATUS/CLASS	Wealthy, Upper Class	Working Class, Poor	Classism
ABILITY/DISABILITY	Temporarily Able-Bodied	People with Disabilities (often physically identifiable)	Ableism
RELIGION	Protestant, Christian	Jewish, Muslim, Hindu, Atheist	Religious Oppression/Intolerance
AGE/GENERATIONAL	Adults (Ages 35-55)	Elders (55+) and Adolescents/Children (25 and under)	Ageism/Adultism

Source: Teaching for Diversity and Social Justice, Second Edition, Routledge, 2007

Could you imagine matrices being created to vilify individuals of African or Muslim heritage? The creators of such a thing would be rightfully denounced.

But this blatant bigotry is proudly displayed by many organizations.

Remember, populations are *never* persuaded to commit atrocities by their leaders declaring, "Let's be evil and harm our innocent neighbors." **Atrocities are committed when people are misled into believing their hatred of another group is *justified*.**

"I don't think identity, *per se*, is necessarily the problem, but it's so much as a victimhood-based identity that gets very radical, where you're all about hating the 'oppressor.' And so you take a very cartoonish view of your enemy as the oppressor, and you dehumanize them."

—*Eric Kaufmann, Canadian professor & author*[68]

MATRIX OF OPPRESSION—BIGOTRY DISGUISED AS "ANTI-BIGOTRY"

As the *Matrix of Oppression* on the facing page shows, institutions now sort human beings into rigid categories of "privileged" (oppressors) and "targeted" (oppressed) based entirely on identity—usually immutable characteristics, sometimes lifestyle choices.

These charts are taught as moral truth, conditioning young and old to believe that moral virtue comes from aligning themselves with an "oppressed" label.

No one absorbs this victimhood matrix more quickly than children and young adults. No young person wants to be labeled an "oppressor" or placed in the "privileged" column, especially when that label comes with social punishment, humiliation, and assumptions of guilt. As a result, many boys and girls will do almost anything to move themselves into an "oppressed" category.

How boys are targeted by the matrix.
Straight, white boys are placed at the very top of the "privileged" column. They are blamed for societal problems they had nothing to do with and bombarded with rhetoric about "toxic masculinity." Normal, healthy masculine traits are vilified, leaving many boys confused, discouraged, and shamed.

How girls are targeted by the matrix.[69]
Girls face different pressures. Simply being female is no longer considered sufficient "victim" status, as shown by their absence from the matrix. Girls quickly learn that identifying as LGBTQQIP2SAA elevates them into a "victim" group. Although feeling pressure to be "L, G, or B" can result in relational discomfort and lifelong regrets, the self-harm from "T" has proven to be the most destructive.

Until very recently, transgender disorders were almost exclusively a male phenomenon. The sudden spike in teen girls and young women identifying as transgender[70] is not the same as these clinical issues—it is a socially-driven choice based partially on the physical discomfort of becoming a woman and the desire to avoid the demonization of being in the "oppressor" column. Tragically today, there's an entire industry of "psychologists" and other "physicians" encouraging these young people to harm themselves based on a demonstrable lie.[71]

Caucasian girls are manipulated from both sides:

A. As a white/Caucasian person, they are placed in the "privileged/oppressor" column;

B. Yet, as women, they are told they are powerless victims of the "patriarchy."

Choosing to be transgender resolves both labels: A. instantly moving these young women into the coveted "oppressed" category, and B. granting them the power to demand that others affirm their self-harm—or face demonization.

The bizarre promotion of transgenderism today is starting in kindergarten[72] and affects both genders.

The tragedy is not only that so many are swept into gender deception, but that their friends and families—believing they are being "loving"—feel pressured to affirm it. There is not a single good thing about a person trying to live as something they will *never* be. Those who express concern or caution are shamed, accused of "bigotry," and told they are causing harm simply for encouraging a young person to accept reality.

Meanwhile, many of these confused young people are being given puberty blockers, testosterone, and irreversible surgeries after only brief consultations by a twisted branch of our medical industry. And, as atrocious as this is, today, formerly respected hospitals and physicians are blatantly lying to young people and their families—not that their child has a clinical condition—but that they are *"actually"* the opposite gender[73] and need immediate life-altering treatment. This is a multi-billion-dollar-a-year industry.[74]

From these treatments, girls can wind up with heightened depression, permanent voice deepening, infertility, facial hair growth, breast removal, sexual dysfunction, menopause symptoms, emotional instability, increased aggression, and a lifelong dependence on medical interventions.[75]

Boys will lose body parts they can never get back. They often face infections and complications from surgeries that attempt to create a non-functional imitation of female anatomy. Far from legitimate medical treatment, these treatments should be viewed as the crimes they are.

Today, political correctness for many—even some parents—outweighs concern for young people doing demonstrable harm to themselves.

Even parents who still live in reality are told that refusing treatment means their child will "likely commit suicide," a frightening claim that pushes parents into submission and plants the dangerous idea into the young person's mind.

Many parents who try to prevent irreversible harm to their children are actually threatened with loss of parental rights. "Trans-influencers" encourage kids to cut off parents who do not affirm their self-harm.

These young people are indeed victims—victims of psychological warfare designed to erode the family unit, redefine truth as subjective, invert morality, and cripple their ability to form the foundational relationships discussed on the previous page.

The idea that the appropriate response to a young person who is either (a) genuinely confused or (b) merely chasing social approval or dodging the "oppressor" label is to guide them toward irreversible bodily harm and mutilation is, again, nothing less than criminal.

To then brand caring family members who resist this harmful nonsense as the true "perpetrators of harm" is one of the clearest examples of how Marxism, moral relativism, and political correctness have inverted moral judgment and are actively destroying lives today.

In the bigger picture, Marxists understand that once a population is conditioned to angrily defend a baseless claim like "gender is a choice," they can be conditioned to accept virtually anything.

As discussed on the facing page, the destruction of gender reality is only one attack on families and societies by neo-Marxist ideologies.

"If you do believe that a man can be a woman, then you are also going to be able to believe that slavery is freedom. That's what they're going after: to erase all kinds of truth."

—Yeonmi Park, American author, human-rights activist & North Korean defector[76]

WHY NEO-MARXIST INSTITUTIONS PROMOTE HARMFUL BEHAVIORS

It's unlikely that anyone will ever love you more than your parents or your spouse. Parental and spousal relationships are the most important in a person's life. These are the individuals to whom you can turn when you need help. They serve as support in difficult times. They will take you in when you have nowhere else to go. They will defend you even when you lack the strength to defend yourself. They will forgive you, and sometimes will even take responsibility for *your* shortcomings.

Upon examination of the objective of Marxist-captured institutions, it becomes clear that the intention is to undermine individuals' capacity to establish these fundamental relationships.

Hook-up culture, false feminism, the "tolerant"—but utterly intolerant—transgender mob,[77] the vilification of hard work, and the abandonment of moral values all contribute to the dismantling of traditional family relationships.

The objective is to cultivate generations of isolated, confused, and unhappy individuals who will be less likely—or less able—to marry and reproduce. Once their parents pass on, they may be—for the most part—alone.

The consequences for these people may be reliance upon an uncaring centralized authority, instead of on a spouse, child, or grandchild who truly cares for them.

What's wrong with individuals who desire this sad outcome for others? Probably sociopathy combined with a hunger for power.

Unfortunately, those with no conscience tend to rise to the top—the *true oppressors* from Formulas 1A and 1B.

But beyond those at the top, the vast majority of people promoting family-destroying narratives have been misled to believe that they are promoting "good" because they no longer employ critical thinking. They follow the group consensus without consideration of the ultimate effect on their lives and the lives of others.

Today, just about all behavior that leads to a healthy traditional family life is demeaned, while behavior that leads ultimately to loneliness is glamorized.

The result is a society that is the pinnacle of technological development and convenience, with a drug-addicted, lonely, confused population who have lost their way.

The road back isn't as far as we think.[78] As stated earlier, we hold the advantage: truth is mightier than lies, and good is easier to defend than evil.

"To rebuild civilization, you must first reclaim your mind—learn to think clearly again; to separate what is from what should be, and what can be done about it. That framework once tethered the West to reality, and without it, chaos reigns.

But ideas alone are not enough. You must reclaim the institutions that shape thought: schools, media, universities, and the churches and the synagogues. They have been captured by those who trade truth for ideology.

The task before you is immense—but it's not yours alone. My generation, and the boomers before it, they owe you. We owe you our help in restoring what we have neglected to preserve for you. A mind that cannot speak cannot think. A nation that cannot debate cannot grow."

—*Ayaan Hirsi Ali, American author, women's-rights activist & survivor of Islamic oppression*[79]

FORMULA 1C

Levels of Corruption

For generations, we've accepted—without question—the practice of electing what Thomas Sowell calls *surrogate decision-makers*.[80] Because nothing says "freedom" like handing your power to strangers.

Even elected or appointed individuals with the best intentions will fall short because one individual can never accurately represent a handful of individuals, let alone the diverse interests and needs of millions.

The stairway below can help students examine who is CORRUPT and to what extent.

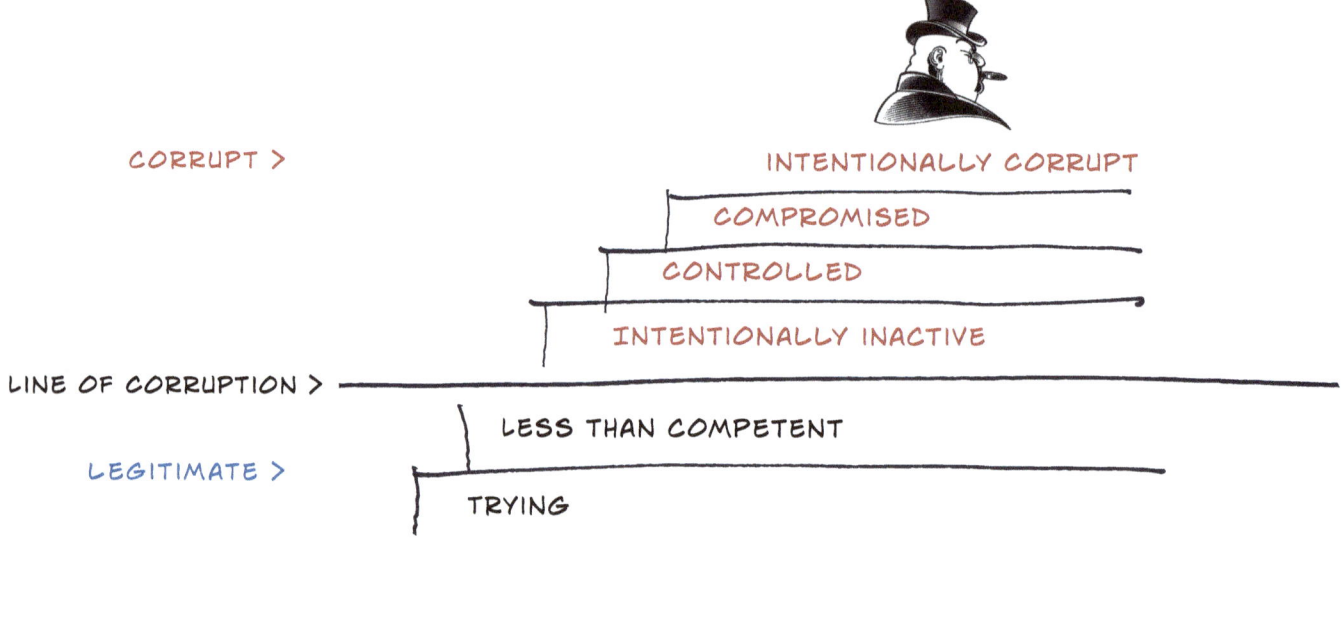

"Among the many dangers of surrogate decision-making is that such decision-makers cannot know the situation of millions of other people as well as those people know their own situations, which may not conform to the vision prevailing among the surrogates.

Moreover, surrogate decision-makers often pay no price for being wrong, no matter how wrong or how catastrophic the consequences for those whose decisions they have preempted.

Given the fallibility of all human beings, the chastening effect of facing the consequences of one's decisions can be dispensed with only at great peril."

—*Thomas Sowell, American economist, economic historian & social theorist* [81]

Surrendering power to a select few all but guarantees corruption. Humans generally care more about themselves and their families than anything else. From hard-core blackmail[86] to the simple threat of loss of employment, concern for one's family can be exploited to draw otherwise decent individuals into corrupt activities.

LEVELS OF AUTHORITY:	WE EXPECT THEIR FOCUS TO BE:	THEIR ACTUAL PRIORITIES:
Global Authorities	The World	Themselves & Their Families
National Authorities	The Country	Themselves & Their Families
State Authorities	The State	Themselves & Their Families
Local Authorities	The Local Community	Themselves & Their Families
Families & Individuals	Themselves & Their Families	Themselves & Their Families

Inspired by Antony Davies, Associate Professor of Economics, Duquesne University[87]

THE REALITY OF CENTRALIZED AUTHORITY

People are always most careful when spending their own hard-earned cash—money that could feed their children. **But today's behemoth U.S. government[83] ensures waste and corruption, because government is spending** *other people's money.*

In our current system, there is little incentive for leadership to represent the taxpayers who *fund* government spending, but every incentive to cater to those who *want the funds*…

Members of Congress are compromised by campaign donations. Government employees can be corrupted with future job offers and payoffs, are nearly impossible to fire,[84] and rarely answer for incompetence or corruption. Today, bureaucratic corruption runs rampant, yet the root problem—our dysfunctional system of electing strangers to make decisions *for us*—goes almost completely unaddressed.

It's time to start having classroom discussions about how we can peacefully disempower corrupt institutions and restore power to the people,[85] as our founders intended.

One solution is illustrated in Formula 2C, starting on page 62.

Solving this problem will not be quick or easy. But every day we delay addressing it is another day lost in defeating corruption and achieving true freedom.

"Nobody spends somebody else's money as carefully as he spends his own."

—*Milton Friedman,*[82] *American economist & educator*

Section 2

FORMULA 2A
How Marxism Destroys

FORMULA 2B
"Enter Through the Narrow Gate..."

FORMULA 2C
Taxpayer Choice & Privatization

FORMULA 2A

How Marxism Destroys

Most people are familiar with the term Marxism, but few understand how it is engineered to destroy. This formula uses compasses to contrast Marxist-influenced vs. traditional societies.

I often wondered as a kid why destructive behavior was being promoted in entertainment and culture and wholesome behavior were being belittled. The answer is Marxism, or "Critical Theory."

Rather than studying society, neo-Marxists' "Critical Theory" seeks to radically alter society by attacking anything constructive or wholesome and tolerating, if not glorifying, that which is destructive.[88]

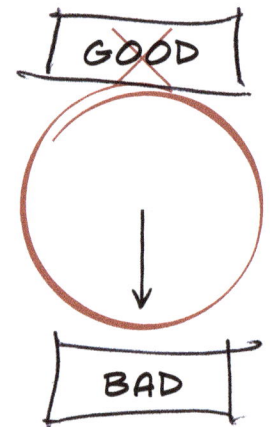
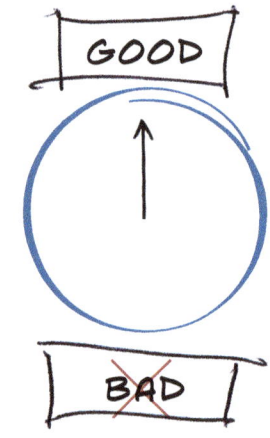

MARXIST SOCIETY

"CRITICAL THEORY"
Good is criticized, bad is glamorized…

SOCIETY DECLINES.

TRADITIONAL SOCIETY

CRITICAL THINKING
Good is promoted, bad is discouraged…

SOCIETY IMPROVES.

All of the behaviors listed on the facing page can be inserted into the *good* or *bad* boxes in the above formula.

"What it basically means is, to change the perception of reality, of every American, to such an extent that despite an abundance of information no one is able to come to sensible conclusions in the interest of defending themselves, their family, their community and their country."

—*Yuri Bezmenov, former KGB agent & Soviet defector* [89]

BAD	GOOD
GLAMORIZED AS "COOL"	BELITTLED AS "CRINGE"
V	V

Sex, drugs & crime	vs.	Wholesome behavior
Single lifestyle	vs.	Marriage & children
Single parenthood	vs.	Two biological parents
"Casual sex" followed by abortion	vs.	Responsibility before sex
Emotion	vs.	Reason
Dressing down	vs.	Dressing with respect
Being overweight	vs.	Being healthy
Climate panic	vs.	Climate reality
Centralized global government	vs.	Government by the people
Gender "fluidity"	vs.	Gender reality
LGBT kids	vs.	LGBT adults only
Gender-neutral parenting	vs.	Parenting based on reality
Men in women's sports	vs.	Women-only sports
Drag queen story hour	vs.	Family-friendly storytelling
Sexualizing children	vs.	Protecting innocence
Encouraging mental illness	vs.	Honesty: "You are not a woman."
Porn as empowerment	vs.	Dignity and modesty
Being defiant at school	vs.	Being a good student
Glamorizing criminals	vs.	Prosecuting criminals
Defunding police	vs.	Funding police
Protecting migrant gangs	vs.	Protecting innocent citizens
Only criminals & government armed	vs.	Legally armed citizens
Illegal migration	vs.	Legal asylum
Open borders	vs.	Secure borders
Mandatory vaccines	vs.	Medical freedom
Equity	vs.	Merit
Universal basic income	vs.	Earned income
Three-tiered justice	vs.	Equal justice under law
"Diversity, equity & inclusion"	vs.	Equal opportunity
Rewriting history	vs.	Honest history
Big government	vs.	Limited government
Bureaucracy	vs.	Free enterprise
Centralized authorities	vs.	Private families
Public housing	vs.	Private property
Censorship	vs.	Free speech
Silencing dissent	vs.	Open debate
Political correctness	vs.	Speaking freely
Hate-speech policing	vs.	First Amendment rights
Surveillance	vs.	Privacy
Socialism	vs.	Capitalism
Hating America	vs.	Loving America
Destroying tradition	vs.	Honoring tradition
Demonizing religion	vs.	Faith & freedom
Etc.		Etc.

Here, too, the sheer volume of inversions is evidence that our society is being manipulated.

"Woe to those who call evil good and good evil, who put darkness for light and light for darkness, who put bitter for sweet and sweet for bitter."—*Isaiah 5:20*

EXAMPLE: GLORIFICATION OF CASUAL SEX & ABORTION

For thousands of years, women and their families required that a young man be a *good man* before he could marry and have sex. This was true feminine empowerment.

Today, women are deceived into believing that having casual sex (the way "men can"), followed by killing the resulting innocent human, is somehow "empowerment." But as usual with Marxist ideals, it's the opposite. It's *surrendering* feminine power.

A society that encourages casual sex followed by abortion is a broken society—and the damage to women and children is staggering.[90]

> "I tell my girls: you have an incredible power on men to elevate their behavior, their choices, their decisions by how you respond to them, okay? It is the soft power that shapes the world, right? That's what women really are—the soft power that shapes the world. Not the dominant, naggy power; the soft, beautiful, alluring power that changes the world."
>
> —Katy Faust, Author & President of Them Before Us [92]

EXAMPLE: PROMOTING & REWARDING SINGLE PARENTHOOD

In decades past, single parenthood was widely condemned, not because people were prudish, but because it is irresponsible to bring a child into the world without two loving parents to raise them.[91]

Today, single moms are placed in the "oppressed" column so even constructive criticism of this irresponsibility is met with hostility.

The U.S. welfare system rewards women for each child they have without a biological father in the home.

How sad to think of little girls growing up without a loving father to tuck them in and protect them—or little boys without a dad to play catch with and teach them responsibility and honor.

EXAMPLE: THE AMERICAN LEFT

By promoting moral inversion and excusing bad behavior, Marxism leaves its adherents with few rational defenses. Lacking facts, they often resort to name-calling. "Racist," "sexist," "homophobe," and "Islamophobe" are not arguments—they're overused insults meant to shame and silence dissent, so destructive ideas can spread unchecked.

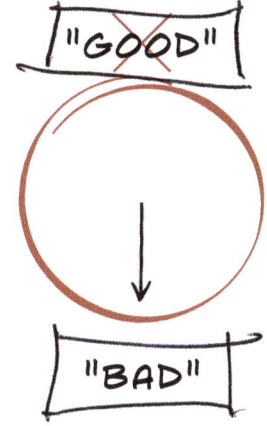

LEFT—MARXIST

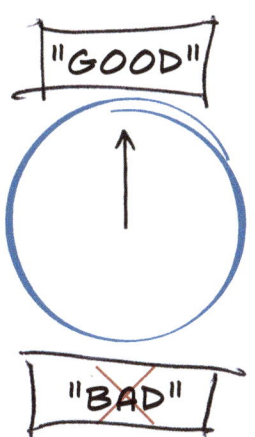

RIGHT—TRADITIONAL

To defend **BAD** and demonize **GOOD**, Marxists must employ:		To encourage **GOOD** and discourage **BAD**, traditional society can stick with:
Lies	vs.	Truth
Feelings	vs.	Facts
Group consensus	vs.	Objective reality
Nonsense	vs.	Common sense
Shaming & fear	vs.	Logic
Inexperience	vs.	Experience
Name-calling	vs.	Addressing the argument
Manipulated data	vs.	Legitimate statistics
Etc.		Etc.

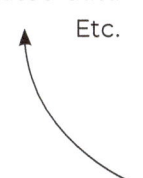

Those who must resort to any of these are rarely defending truth or decency.

Ironically, the Left believes the Right are *evil*. The Right believes the Left are *misled*.

The asymmetry is important: one side sees the other as *hateful bigots;* the other side sees the first as merely *deceived*. The first view morally justifies vitriol and retaliation; the second permits persuasion, honest debate, and the possibility of recovery.

So, if one side believes their opponents are villains, while the other believes their opponents are victims of malicious disinformation, who are truly the "hateful bigots?"

The "oppressed vs. oppressor" groups from page 29 can also be inserted into Formula 2A. A few examples are shown on these two pages. Unlike the *behaviors* on the previous page, most *groups* are not inherently "good" or "bad"; rather, *conditions* for one group are portrayed as better or worse than for another—whether true or not.

MARX'S ORIGINAL OPPRESSED VS OPPRESSOR NARRATIVE

Marx's theory was economic. His ideas falsely claim to be "for the workers" (proletariat) and against the business owners (bourgeois). But in practice, Marxism undermines both business owners and workers while empowering free society's true adversaries—the corrupt centralized authorities shown in Formulas 1A-1C.

This is the destructive pattern applied to anything Marxists want to destroy.

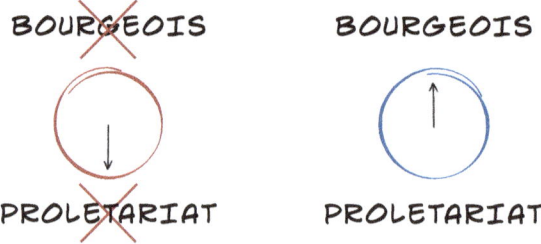

FREE NATIONS UNDER ATTACK

Free nations—with the greatest middle-class prosperity in human history—are smeared by Marxists as "racist" and flooded with migrants from struggling nations, harming both.[93] Free nations are overwhelmed; struggling nations are stripped of their most driven citizens.[94]

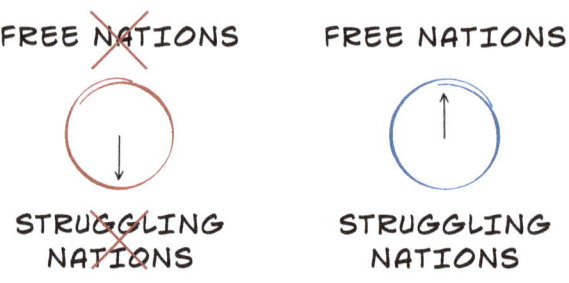

DEMONIZATION OF LAW ENFORCEMENT

The media demonizes law enforcement, turning weak-minded viewers against the very people they would call in an emergency. Meanwhile, it excuses criminals as "victims" while actual victims are dismissed, forgotten, or even blamed. This harms everyone, including the criminals.

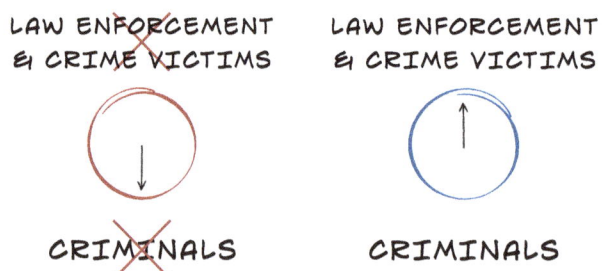

Far from "helping the downtrodden," neo-Marxist narratives always harm both groups—and society in general.

THE TRAGIC DEATH OF SCOUTING
Rather than working to improve the Girl Scouts, Marxists encouraged girls to guilt their way into the Boy Scouts—ironically ending the very institution they were so eager to join and weakening their own organization by abandoning it.

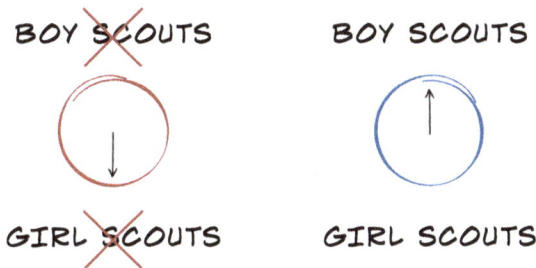

LGBT KIDS & GENDER NONSENSE
LGBT children's parades and drag queen story hour—far from being the "tolerant" and "loving" events they claim to be—harm children by confusing them with adult activities at inappropriate ages. This can fuel *groomer* stereotypes about the LGBT community.

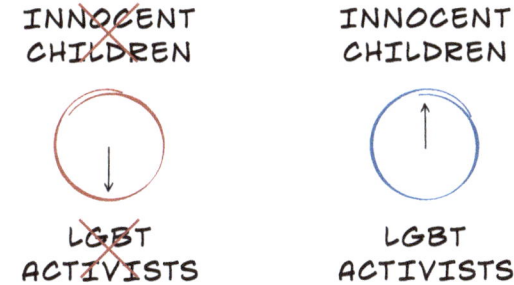

ATTACK ON FAMILIES
Marxism seeks government control—strong families stand in its way. Belittling marriage, confusing gender roles, normalizing promiscuity and abortion, and pushing LGBT agendas make forming loving, lifelong relationships more difficult. Without family to turn to, people are more likely to become dependent on the state.

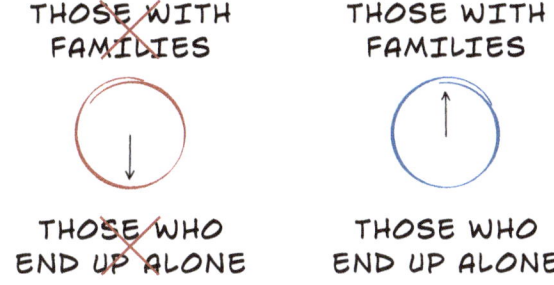

THE TREMENDOUS SUCCESS OF MARXIST DEMORALIZATION THROUGH MEDIA AND ACADEMIA IN THE U.S.

If we ever recover from the psychological warfare we are subject to today, some of what occurred will need to be recorded—because it is so ridiculous that, thinking people of the future may hardly believe it…

- Divisions are being propagated—wherever possible—between demographic groups not only in America but around the world.

- Forgoing common sense and experience, otherwise intelligent individuals were convinced to walk around in public wearing surgical masks.[95] Those who didn't were subjected to hostility.

- Millions of Americans faced job loss for refusing experimental genetic therapy the media called a "vaccine." Although it allegedly protected only its recipients from infection, hostility toward the "unvaxxed" was unprecedented, and many were banned or even publicly shamed for declining the injection.

- The fear induced by corrupt institutions over a virus resulted in the unprecedented erosion of human rights and business freedoms.

- One of the most powerful and wealthy women in the world funded a website entitled *Shout Your Abortion*. The site offers customized T-shirts that a woman can purchase to celebrate the number of her own offspring that she has killed.[96]

- Adult LGBT sex is being celebrated in grade schools and at children's parades.[97]

- Corrupt institutions have convinced some parents, teachers, and even doctors that they are "virtuous" for telling children they can "choose their gender." Not only is it a lie, but it can lead to irreversible mutilation, life-altering hormones, and difficulty forming important familial relationships. This is intended to create a generation of lonely, angry individuals who will be reliant on the medical system and on the government.[98]

- Formerly respected hospitals—including Boston Children's, Johns Hopkins, the Mayo Clinic, and many more—are engaging in mutilation of children (and adults) based on the lie that gender can be altered.[99] These hospitals have asked the U.S. Department of Justice to investigate those who voice opposition to their programs.[100]

- A nominee for associate justice of the Supreme Court could not define what a woman is during her confirmation hearing.[101]

- Biological men are being welcomed by sports organizations to compete against female athletes, essentially stealing their trophies and their ability to qualify for scholarships. Those female athletes who express opposition to this situation are subjected to offers of "therapy" to help them overcome their "trans-phobia."[102]

- Biological men are being permitted in locker rooms where women and little girls are changing into and out of clothing and bathing suits. Women who complain about this have their memberships canceled and are banned from the facility, while fetishist, mentally ill men are permitted to continue to violate women's spaces.[103]

- An actor was banned from hosting readings of his wholesome children's book, *As You Grow*,[104] at over 50 publicly funded libraries[105]—despite many hosting *drag queen story hour* and offering deviant sex books like *Gender Queer: A Memoir*.[106]

- In many classrooms, kids who study are mocked, and kids who disrupt are indulged—because "standards" are now considered oppressive.

- The UK is arresting roughly 12,000 of its own citizens every year for social media posts expressing concern over immigrant gang assaults on women and the mutilation of children based on the idea that gender is "fluid."[107]

- Destructive behavior—such as crime and drug use—is tolerated and often glamorized. Society's successful traditions—such as traditional families, wholesome behavior, and gender roles based on reality—have been demonized based on the Marxist agenda that states: society must be torn down so that it can be "built back better."[108]

- Mainstream media is intentionally stoking hatred of law enforcement, such as ICE, who risk their lives to arrest drug-cartel members, human traffickers, rapists, and murderers. At the same time, they displace blame and often *excuse* violent criminals.

- Students are being taught to be hateful of the United States and that the U.S. is "racist."

- Those who reside in safe white communities are demanding that the police be *defunded* while they claim to care about those who reside in high-crime communities.[109]

- Guns are blamed for actions committed by criminals in an attempt to demonize law-abiding Americans' right to bear arms. Loss of Americans' 2nd-Amendment rights would leave only the government and criminals with weapons.

- Rather than prioritizing educational improvement, some educators and schools promote transgender nonsense, and racial division.[110]

- In 2025, about two-thirds of public-school students aren't reading at a proficient level, and roughly 40% of 4th-graders fall below even the basic benchmark. In 2022, just 26 percent[111] of 8th-grade public schoolers reached NAEP Proficiency in math—despite the United States outspending most of the developed world on education.[112]

- Colleges—far from teaching the value of free speech—silence and ban speakers and educators who do not agree with today's far-left narratives.[113] Many now have "free speech zones," a 4-ft-by-4-ft square where non-woke speech is allowed.[114]

- Classes such as "feminist studies" and "gender studies" are often required in today's universities, regardless of your degree program. They teach no legitimate skills; instead, they cultivate resentment, division, and a sense of victimhood. Graduates of these "woke" majors face limited job prospects—apart from returning to academia to pass the same destructive ideas on to the next generation.

- Hatred of the successful and hardworking is increasingly taught in schools, and ambition is routinely belittled. Meanwhile, drug addiction, voluntary homelessness, and crime are tolerated and solutions are seldom explored.

The influence of Marxism has made our society unrecognizable in just two generations...

grandparents

DEMARXIFICATION—PAGE 46

grandkids

Why have we allowed this to happen?

What is wrong with the corrupt individuals who want this for society?

DEMARXIFICATION—PAGE 48

MARXISM IS HYPOCRISY

Another mechanism of Marxism is that it is engineered to make its followers hypocrites—guilty of the very accusations they level against others:

- Leftists falsely demonize their opposition as "haters," while the act of labeling someone a "hater" is hateful in itself.
- Forcing pronoun compliance under threat of being labeled "intolerant" is itself intolerant.
- Saying "all white people are racist" is racist.
- Forbidding criticism of non-whites ironically echoes white supremacy by assuming whites can handle jokes and critique, while "poor" minorities are "beneath us," so we shouldn't say anything about them.
- Diversity policies are created to be "anti-racist," yet determining "diversity" requires judging people by skin color—which is blatantly racist.

No one does hypocrisy better than modern "feminists," who:

- Disdain traditional feminine roles and femininity.
- Disparage men and their roles, yet glorify masculine roles for women.
- Tolerate men destroying women's sports.
- Encourage casual sex and abortion as somehow "empowering" for women (as if men really hate this—you show 'em, girls!).

As a woman, I am embarrassed by what many women have become and the often foolish narratives they champion.

If "feminists" ever bothered to critically evaluate the causes they are urged to support—rather than mindlessly conforming to groupthink—their contributions might become meaningful instead of harmful.

In a true vision of feminism, women would use their femininity to inspire and motivate men. Instead of demeaning men—and striving to compete with them in male roles—women would encourage men to work hard, solve problems, and be good husbands and fathers.

Imagine the good that could be done if women volunteered to help children, read to the elderly, rescue helpless animals, or pursue any number of productive endeavors. Instead, they are deceived into funneling their anger, time, and energy into demanding the right to kill their own innocent offspring without apology—the least "feminine" action one can take.

While "feminists" encourage women to poorly occupy male roles, feminine *caring* roles—so vital to society—go neglected. Children are relegated to centralized schools, the elderly are often lonely and isolated, and social challenges such as drug addiction, mental illness, and homelessness persist.

THE HYPOCRISY BUILT INTO MARXIST RULE—RULES FOR THEE, NOT FOR ME

In practice, Marxist leaders do not participate in the food rationing or forced labor that they impose on their own people. The Marxist elite enjoy commerce—but only through corruption. What is known as the "black market" is not "free" enterprise; it is privilege reserved for the powerful.

Black marketeers can earn extra money—unlike the rest of the population—but only if they are protected by the corrupt regime, or if they manage not to be caught.

Thus, even under communism, the entrepreneurial spirit survives; it's simply driven underground into utter corruption.

As usual, the polar opposite of its promises, Marxism recreates the very hierarchy it claims to oppose: commerce is permitted only for the ruling elite and their loyal minions. Average citizens engaging in free trade in places like North Korea or the former Soviet Union would be imprisoned or executed.[115]

FORMULA 2B
"Enter through the narrow gate..." —Matthew 7:13

Many well-intentioned individuals—including professors, friends, and even parents—are being manipulated through multiple avenues into promoting harmful ideas.

Formula 2B contains both compasses from the Formula 2A but expands the negative (red) moral compass into the four red compasses that are flanking the center compass below. Plotting individuals, entities, ideas, and more on the landscape below can help us define, clarify, and question their influence.

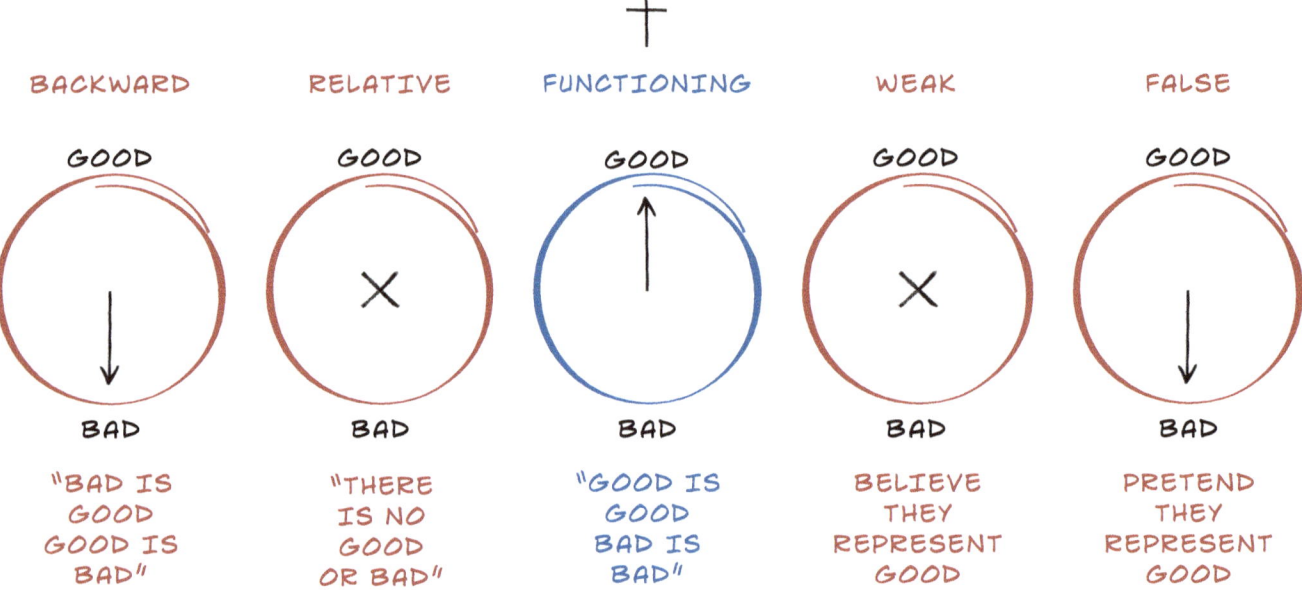

Although God is the ultimate authority over all truth, the information we receive in this construct generally comes through human channels—whether parents, media, or the writers of the Bible.

We can plot individuals on the landscape above—those we know personally as well as public figures—to evaluate how each influences our own direction or the direction of others.

We detail each compass in the rest of the chapter...

THE FUNCTIONING MORAL COMPASS

In a culture that's been heavily influenced by backward Marxist thinking, we find it necessary to state the obvious. As discussed in the simpler version—Formula 2A in the previous chapter—in a society with a Functioning Moral Compass, *good* is promoted and *bad* is discouraged.

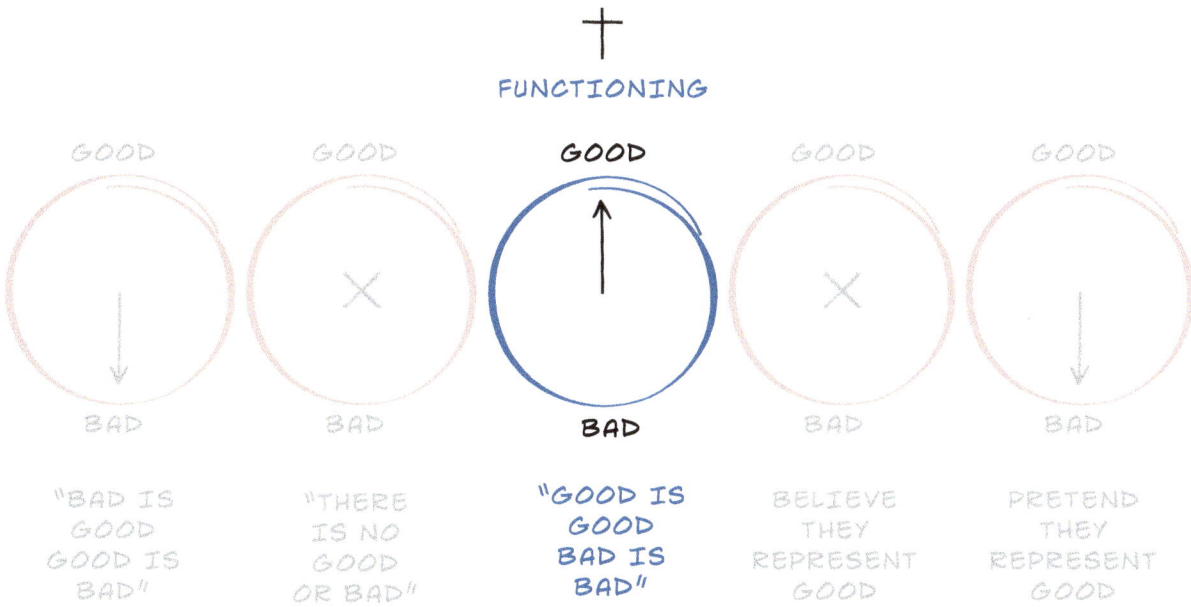

An individual, idea, or institution that follows this compass will be doing their best to help themselves, their families, and their communities.

They will seldom get it completely right—represented by the omni-directional compass hands below—but they will try to the best of their ability.

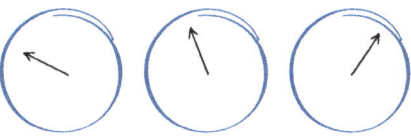

Only Jesus can be described as the perfect due-north-facing compass. The rest of us are sinners.

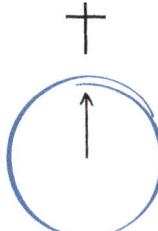

"But you know that he appeared so that he might take away our sins. And in him is no sin."—*1 John 3:5*

THE RELATIVE MORAL COMPASS

This is the most dangerous compass on the landscape. Those who follow this compass believe that they are the "epitome of righteousness."

Relativism is the belief that "tolerance" is the supreme virtue and that "there is no good or bad; it's all 'relative' to the individual or group." Like most Marxist ideals, it sounds noble but is profoundly destructive, persuading people that tolerating evil is a good thing.

The irony, of course, is that the ever-so-"tolerant" relativists are completely *intolerant* of those who strive to discern right from wrong as illustrated on the previous page. This reflects the Marxist doctrine of *repressive tolerance*,[116] which amounts to tolerating only those who *agree* with you.

Relativists also apply their "tolerance" differently to those labeled "oppressed" versus those labeled "oppressors," from Formula 1B. This is why we see American leftists excusing wrongdoing by culpable groups while imposing guilt on innocent ones.

As illustrated in Formula 2A and elsewhere in the program, Marxist narratives harm everyone involved. Excusing crime, of course, harms victims and the broader community—but it also harms the criminals themselves.

EXAMPLE 1:

Muslims are placed in the "oppressed" row, so their history[117] and questionable customs are excused by the relativist-influenced left. Practices such as forced marriage,[118] female genital mutilation,[119] *taharrush*,[120] and *bacha bazi*[121] are minimized, denied, or tolerated under the guise of "someone else's culture." Apostates who speak out—even victims of these practices[122]—are subject to hate-filled rhetoric and live under threat of death.

If American rednecks practiced forced marriages, honor killings, polygamy, or female genital mutilation, they'd be rightly condemned.

EXAMPLE 2:

Because the LGBT community is in the "oppressed" row, they are permitted to hold children's events celebrating their sexuality. Imagine if heterosexuals celebrated sex in the presence of children, with rainbows, unicorns, face-painting, dancing cartoon characters, and so forth.

Leftists enthusiastically support such events while demonizing those in opposition with labels like "homophobic," "transphobic," or simply "hateful." Name-calling is commonly used by the left to defend destructive ideas, as discussed on page 41 and in the ancillary formulas.

The Relative Moral Compass—far from the moral high ground it claims—is one of the most damaging belief systems in human history.

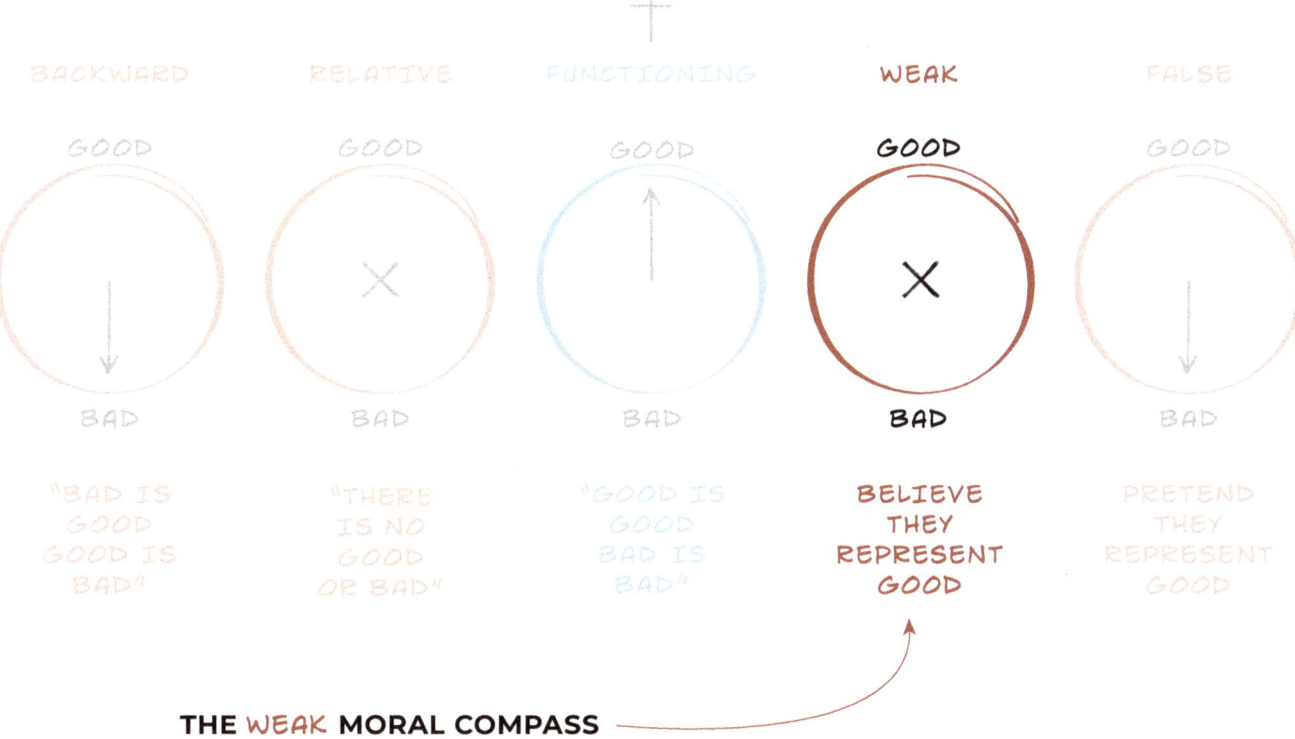

THE WEAK MORAL COMPASS

Just as with the compass on the facing page, those we plot on this compass sincerely believe their actions are righteous. But whereas moral relativists reject the idea of objective right and wrong, these individuals do judge right from wrong—but through a flawed lens that leads to uncharitable methods. As a result, they often produce the opposite of the good they intend.

EXAMPLE 1
In a political discussion, Sen. Joseph McCarthy was correct to oppose communism. But the witch hunt he carried out in the early 1950s made opposition to communism unpopular. "McCarthyism" ultimately boosted communism's image and caused those who rightfully oppose it to appear intolerant.[123]

EXAMPLE 2
In a discussion of religion, this compass would apply to sanctimonious Christians—those who truly believe they are doing God's work but whose overly dogmatic behavior contradicts Christ's example and casts Christianity in a negative light.

"You tell people that you love how to avoid the road to hell. And you don't do that because you're shaking your finger at them, or because you're a 'moral authority.'

You do it because you don't want them to burn…

And I think there's too much of the 'moral authority' still in the church, and not enough of the, you know, the love that helps people avoid the fire."

—*Dr. Jordan B. Peterson, Canadian psychologist, author & educator*[124]

THE BACKWARD MORAL COMPASS

Unlike those following the compasses on the previous two pages, who believe they are doing good, someone knowingly—and unapologetically—espousing evil would be plotted under this compass.

This includes your psychopath, your narcissist, your cult leader, and occasionally—your teenager(!).

Charles Manson and Aleister Crowley would fall under this compass.

THE FALSE MORAL COMPASS

Someone following this compass is *knowingly* doing harm but outwardly pretending to be on the side of good.

Priests who molest children or televangelists who only *pretend* to be Christians to gain wealth and power would fall under the False Moral Compass.

Purely hypothetically, if Sen. Joe McCarthy in the previous example was not *sincerely* opposed to communism—but secretly intended to bolster sympathy for communism—he would also fall under this compass in a discussion of politics of his time.

Few follow the False and Backward Compasses. Those with Relative and Weak Compasses are vastly more numerous than the blatantly evil demon-worshipers, or the falsely virtuous televangelists who can both come across as silly.

Author's Testimony:

My apologies to both atheists and Christians.

Atheists—I'm sorry that you live in a Darwinian nightmare full of sorrow, hate, abuse, and heartbreak... followed by death... Bummer for you.

Christians—please forgive me. My path to Jesus was somewhat unorthodox.

I admire those who found Christ through faith and family. It must have been wonderful to know the unconditional love of Jesus as a child and throughout one's life. My 1970s Pennsylvania Catholic Sunday school didn't exactly light any fires.

No, my journey to Christianity began only recently from listening to a panel that discussed a *literal* belief in creation.[125] It seems that both the Bible—and science—support the likelihood that we live in a designed construct,[126] not a Darwinian accident.

I understand that, as Jesus said, "Blessed are those who have not seen and yet have believed" (John 20:29). But I can't change the means by which I found my belief and faith in Jesus. And today, with Darwinian evolution taught as the prevailing "scientific" consensus and the wisdom of the Bible largely excluded from public education, I hope my experience might help others discover belief in Jesus as I did—through a scientific understanding of creation. As far as I'm concerned, any path that can lead to Him is a good thing.

In reality, we all know that the Darwinian hypothesis isn't exactly scientific.

The notion that life simply "sprang from a lifeless planet" is something even your grade-school teachers admit humans have *never* observed in nature or replicated in a lab. Then, the idea that an individual spark of life evolved into the vast array of organisms—plants, animals, insects, and so on—seems like a far-fetched fairy tale.

Truly—I'm embarrassed that I fell for it. But since we are taught this at such a young age, we do not question it. The result...

For those taught to believe in evolution—the accidental appearance of life—the universe has no purpose, we have no purpose, we are fancy monkeys allegedly whizzing through space at imperceptible speeds, and then we die... joy, joy.

What a bleak outlook to teach children. No wonder so many in our society are depressed and hopeless.

For those taught to believe that life and the universe were *created*, then the universe has a purpose, life has a purpose, and an adventure awaits each of us.[127]

A graphic designer by trade—a "creator" myself—the next logical step in my thinking was to begin comparing human creations to the divine creation that we inhabit.

Genetic commonality in lifeforms alone proves nothing. Yes, chimpanzees and humans share about 98.8% of their DNA—but if I animated a human and a chimp, their computer code would look a heck of a lot alike too.

Beyond taking the wind out of evolution, comparing human and divine creations can also help answer some of Christianity's most difficult questions, such as: Why would a benevolent God allow bad things to happen? How can God forgive those who have done horrible things? How can the universe be only 6,000 years old? I speculate on these and other questions in an article on the program's website linked here. >

Continued...

Genesis reads like a checklist for a GDD (game design document). First, create the environment: lighting, heaven and earth, land and sea, flora and fauna. Then create the main characters and breathe life into an actual player—Adam.

From the beauty and diversity of animal life to the intricacies of beneficial bacteria, would anyone create a universe of such staggering complexity without a purpose?

Do humans create video games where players are fed grapes and fanned with palm fronds all day? Of course not. There's always something to achieve, a challenge to overcome, or villains to defeat.

Perhaps our life on earth is one big education.

You've likely heard the phrase "youth is wasted on the young." Well... imagine living an entire lifetime within this construct—gaining faith, wisdom, perspective, and clarity—then returning to your loved ones in heaven—renewed—and carrying the wisdom of a centenarian.

We could tell those who loved us—whom we were too young or ungrateful to fully appreciate—how much they meant to us, and make right in heaven what we got wrong on earth.

I can't imagine a better education.

Those unfamiliar with the Bible often believe that God is some kind of "authoritarian," telling us what to do. But God's edicts are not for *God's* benefit—they are for *ours*. The Christian Bible is the best guide for navigating both life and this creation. Its supernatural wisdom and complexity are unparalleled.[128]

Unfortunately, our society is being led away from this glorious light and toward profound darkness.

Instead of the wisdom of the Bible, today, there are grade schools celebrating deviant sex.[129] People who profess to be the epitome of "tolerance" are openly hateful toward Christians, free countries, heterosexuals, white people, and men. Bad behavior is celebrated, and good behavior is disdained.

This is not normal.

The sheer existence of these dark, nonsensical narratives furthers my belief that we are in a construct—because the powerful individuals pushing this destruction cannot possibly be so obtuse. They must know that when they harm society, they harm themselves. "A rising tide lifts all boats."[130] So why are powerful people so bent on society's destruction?

Are they simply this construct's BBEGs (Big Bad Evil Guys), and it's our challenge to defeat them?

In any case, these narratives must be actively dismantled. Education is where Marxists begin their work—and it is where we must begin ours.

If we start teaching children from a young age to be *good people,* to help others, to act with integrity, and love their neighbors, what an amazing world this would be. This is how a society can be restored—it's not rocket science—simply teach the wisdom of the Bible.

We are not defenseless against those who seek to turn our society from the light. Jesus has our backs. He loves us. He is our Savior, our protector, and with Him, we need not fear.

May His blessings be with you.

"Yea, though I walk through the valley of the shadow of death, I will fear no evil: for thou art with me; thy rod and thy staff they comfort me.."—*Psalm 23:1–4*

Bad "Freedom"

Good Freedom

DEMARXIFICATION—PAGE 58

GOOD FREEDOM—BAD "FREEDOM"

In Formulas 1A and 1B *freedom* is the objective, freedom is good.
In Formulas 2A and 2B "*freedom*" or "anything goes," is *not* good.

As illustrated on page 14, the English language has few words for freedom.
It is important to discern *good* freedom from *bad* freedom.

Simplified Formulas 1A/1B :

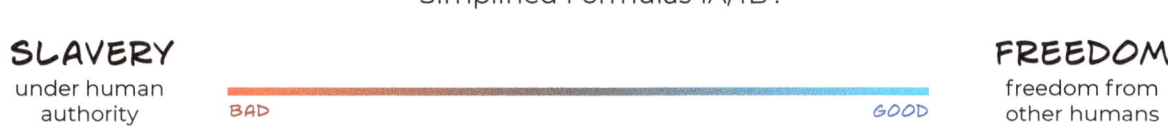

The freedom referred to on the scale above is freedom from *slavery* or from *exploitation*—this is good.

The "freedom" referred to on the scale below is "freedom" from *morality*—this is not good.

Abbreviated Formulas 2A/2B:

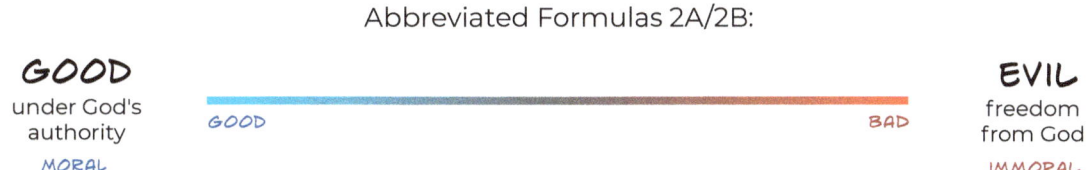

Being "free" from morality is not genuine freedom, but enslavement to immoral habits.
Being free from corrupt individuals who wish to exploit others is the freedom we want.

Today's left intentionally inverts both of these. They have been misled to believe that populations and economies should be controlled by centralized authority, and that morality should be "anything goes."

This is commonly known as the "alignment chart" in the context of tabletop role-playing games, particularly Dungeons & Dragons.

But I'm going to use the terms: "freedom, slavery, good and evil," from the formulas.

Note... if the center position is the desired position on these two charts, then the above is **not** what we want for our purposes.

The last thing we want is to be halfway good, and halfway free!

The solution is to go back to the long form of both formulas where the desired outcome is represented in the center...

FORMULA 1A

FORMULA 2B

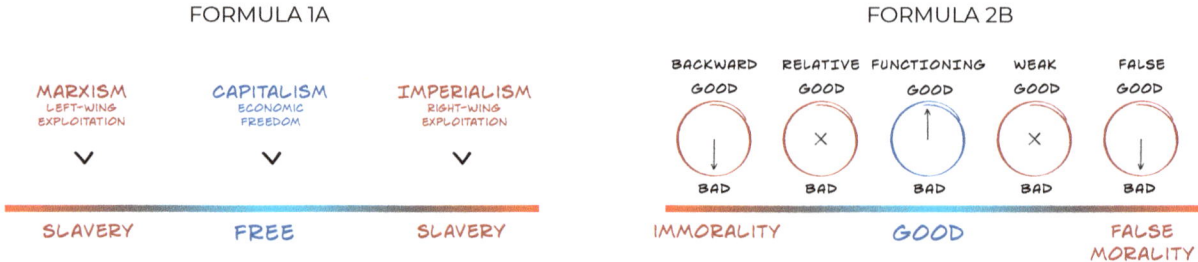

When the lines beneath these two formulas above are crossed, they translate to this below, with the desired outcome in the middle and negative influences on all four sides...

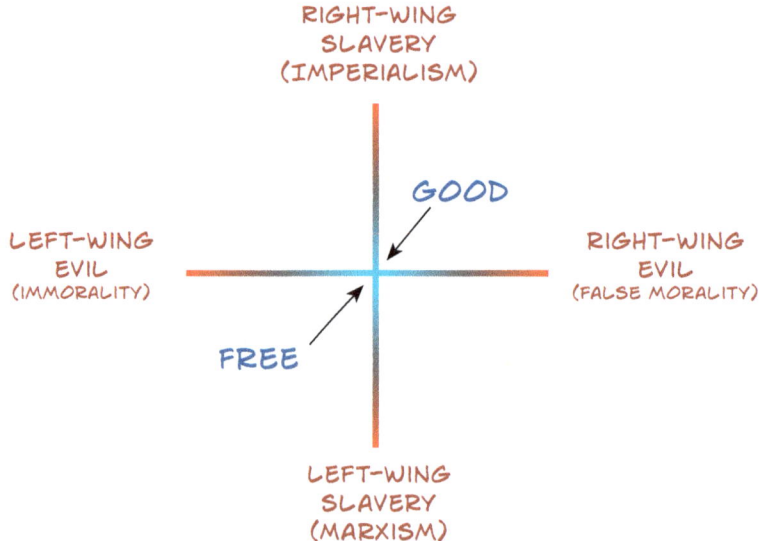

DEMARXIFICATION—PAGE 60

...but raising the blue area into a 3D pyramid may illustrate it best:

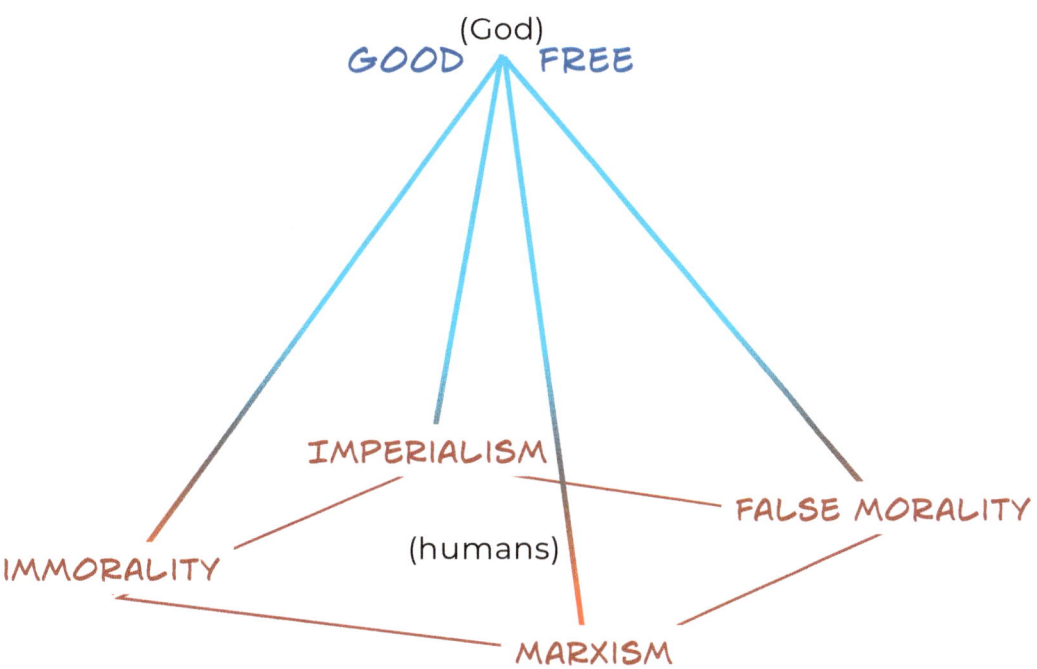

As the saying goes, "You know you're over the target when they're shooting at you from all sides."

"For my thoughts are not your thoughts, neither are your ways my ways," declares the LORD. "As the heavens are higher than the earth, so are my ways higher than your ways and my thoughts than your thoughts."—Isaiah 55:8–9

"It is better to take refuge in the LORD than to trust in humans. It is better to take refuge in the LORD than to trust in princes."—Psalm 118:8–9 (NIV)

FORMULA 2C

Taxpayer Choice & Privatization

Giving 535 members of Congress the power to decide what to do with massive amounts of *other people's money* is ludicrous—and always has been.

This formula reveals paths to solving society's deepest problems.

Though we lack the education and truthful media needed to implement such changes now, discussing alternatives is the first step toward a future where power truly lies with the people.

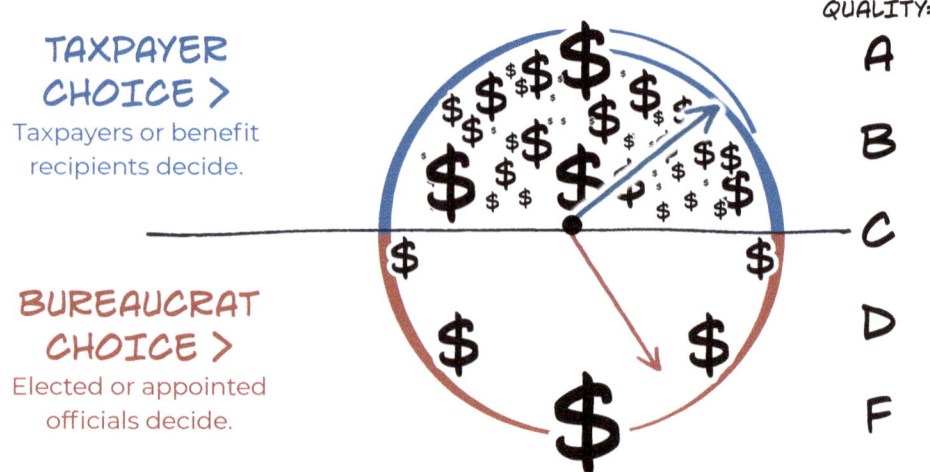

TAXPAYER CHOICE >
Taxpayers or benefit recipients decide.

BUREAUCRAT CHOICE >
Elected or appointed officials decide.

QUALITY:
A
B
C
D
F

HOW TO FUND COLLECTIVE NEEDS WITHOUT "SURROGATE DECISION-MAKERS":

THE PROBLEM: BUREAUCRAT CHOICE
The American Revolution was launched over a 1–2% tax by the British Empire. Today, Americans can be taxed up to 37% under threat of prison, with no say in how the money is spent. Is this actually *freedom,* or is it oppressive imperialism? And the Federal Reserve is a sneaky tax that has devalued our dollars by 97% since its inception.[131]

Why do we tolerate this? Because powerful NGOs keep young activists busy with transgender bathrooms and hatred of law enforcement instead of organizing against our true enemy—corruption.

I would say our system is "broken" but that's wrong. "Broken" would mean it once functioned. This system was dysfunctional from the start. Far from representing citizens, our "representatives" bow to campaign donors. It's time to imagine alternatives...

THE SOLUTION: TAXPAYER CHOICE
Citizens still vote and pay taxes, but instead of rubber-stamping omnibus bills rife with corruption and waste, elected individuals manage a system of *vouchers* in which *citizens choose* where their tax dollars are allocated.

Would the gravy train of funding for illegals, bureaucratic kickback projects—and even many foreign wars—keep rolling if American taxpayers could say "no" and keep more of their money to use for their own families?

Through *taxpayer choice,* bureaucrats are put in their place, families are empowered, and corruption is vastly more difficult to achieve.

On the following pages, we examine how this works in the case of the FDA, education, and welfare.

EXAMPLE: SWITZERLAND
Switzerland holds up to four national votes per year—from environmental regulations to economic reforms. Citizens reject a majority of the initiatives.

EXAMPLE: FOOD & DRUG ADMINISTRATION

The conflict of interest in the "Food & Drug Administration" is evident in its *name*. For decades now, the FDA has allowed *food* companies to sell products linked to long-term illness while allowing *drug* companies to sell solutions for the resulting health problems.

When pharmaceutical, food, and medical institutions answer not to the public but to bureaucrats with deep ties to the very industries they regulate, corruption becomes predictable. Future job offers, stock options, and other incentives are commonplace. And—because these institutions are government-imposed monopolies—we cannot fire them or choose another option.

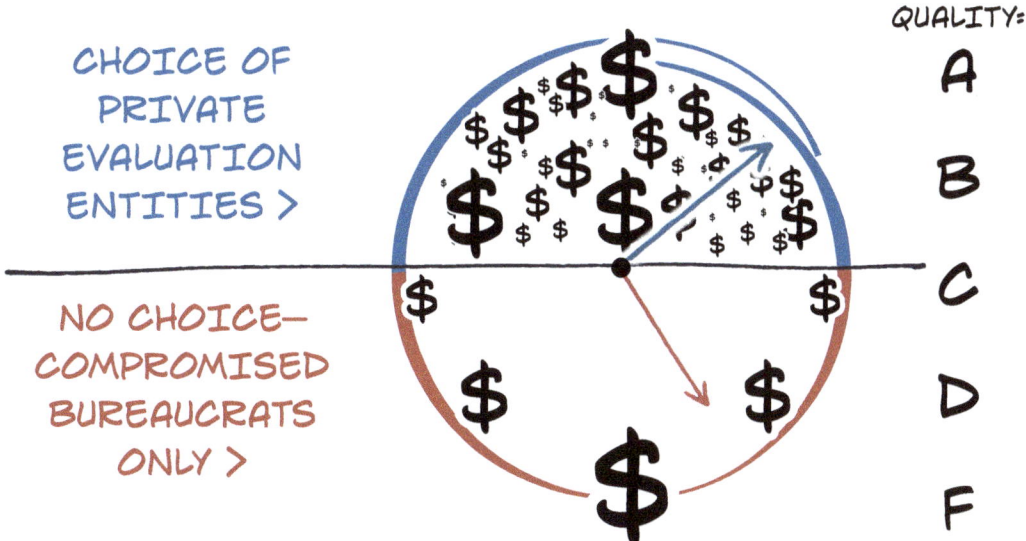

"But whatever would we do without the FDA? We don't have the time or expertise to research food ingredients for ourselves!"

The solution is simple—what did people do in centuries past? *When they handed someone their hard-earned cash, they relied on the integrity of the seller to provide quality items.*

If the FDA disappeared overnight, entrepreneurs would rush to fill the gap. Private companies would offer analyses of food from reputable institutions and translate them for public understanding.

To assure customers that their food is of quality, grocery stores would pay for these independent evaluations, and companies would compete for the contracts. One might offer a kiosk-based scanner, another a smartphone app, and yet another might offer a color-coded labeling system. Consumers would select the store with the system they prefer.

If one rating agency's credibility becomes tarnished, a switch to an alternative is possible—a flexibility that doesn't exist under monopolies like the FDA, which may range from do-nothing to corrupt.

Again, we can't fire the FDA and choose a less corrupt service to ensure food safety. This highlights the importance of institutional privatization, competition, and *choice* whenever feasible.

There is no freedom without choice...

"If a private organization does things badly, it will lose money and have to go out of business.
If a public organization does things badly—it will be expanded."

—*Milton Friedman*[132]

EXAMPLE: K-12 EDUCATION

Our current educational systems are the worst of both worlds: private schools for only the very wealthy, and public schools for everyone else.

The answer to this is *educational competition*.

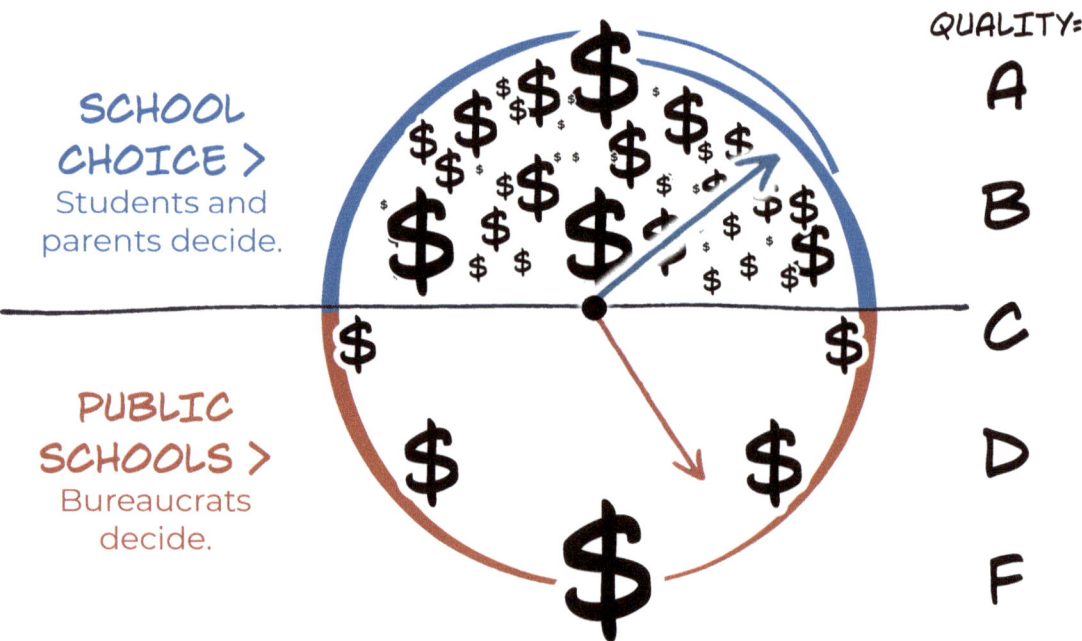

PUBLIC SCHOOLS— POOR EDUCATION FOR ALL

In public schools, children attend school in their zip code. Equal education for all? Hardly. Schools in wealthy areas thrive while schools in poor communities fall behind. But parents don't have a choice; this system is run by uncaring bureaucrats and school boards.

And in the bureaucrats' wisdom—as shown on the bottom of this formula—the worse a school performs, the more money it receives.

Because nothing says "success" like rewarding failure.[133]

SCHOOL CHOICE— PRIVATE SCHOOLS FOR ALL

In a voucher system—"school choice" or "private school for all"—each school-age child receives a voucher of equal value, earmarked for education expenses only.

These vouchers can be used in the *free-market* with options such as private schools, tutors, homeschooling, and most importantly—*apprenticeships,* detailed on the facing page.

> "Successful education shows what is possible, whether in charter schools, private schools, military schools, or homeschooling. The challenge is to provide more escape hatches from failing public schools, not only to help those students who escape, but also to force these institutions to get their act together before losing more students and jobs."
>
> —*Thomas Sowell*

THE BENEFITS OF A VOUCHER-BASED SYSTEM:

Control of children's education would lie completely with the family, rather than with uncaring school boards or bureaucrats.

PRIVATE SCHOOLS FOR ALL:

- "Woke" schools would have to compete with classical and specialized educational programs for vouchers and additional funding. Good schools would flourish, bad schools would close, all based on the choices of *students and parents*.

- Many private and charter schools such as Acton Academy[134] or Michaela Community School[135] would offer opportunities beyond the traditional classroom—paid for by vouchers.

- The competitive privatization of schools would also result in competition for the best teachers. Consequently, education would become a lucrative career path offering more than just higher teaching salaries. It would encourage educational *entrepreneurship*, with opportunities for teachers to establish schools or even franchises.

- Former public school buildings can offer rooms to be rented by educators using a portion of the proceeds from the vouchers.

- Part of the voucher's value can pay for students' use of sports facilities, for participation in team activities, even lunches and social functions.

- And much more...

APPRENTICESHIPS:

- Throughout most of human history, apprenticeships were the common practice. While children might learn basic reading, writing, and arithmetic in a school setting, their education continued with hands-on training in the real world.

- This creates higher adult-to-student ratios with many adults in the community playing an active role in educating the youth.

- Tax dollars, instead of going to bureaucracy, would be a huge boost to businesses throughout the community.

- Businesses receive payment for training young individuals *and* benefit from the work they complete.

- Students gain invaluable experience of working in a professional setting with experienced adults.

- A soft landing for young people into the working world: Hazing or mistreatment of "the new guy" would disappear. Instead, business owners would be incentivized to ensure that their employees take voucher participants under their wing for mentorship.

- Apprentices who work hard may receive employment offers—or even funding for further education—from the company.

- And much more...

Apprenticeships would give colleges and universities a run for their money.

This shift could lead to major reforms in higher education such as the death of useless majors, such as feminist and gender studies.

Degree programs—dictated by professors who may never have held a job in the real world—would give way to *à la carte* instruction from real-world employers.

OBJECTIONS TO VOUCHER SYSTEMS STEM FROM IGNORANCE.

The word *voucher* has been demonized. Many people believe that vouchers are for "rich people who want a discount on private school." This misconception stems from the belief that student choices would be limited to *existing schools only*—which, in most communities, means the local public school system and perhaps a private—usually Catholic—school.

If this were the case, it would indeed be unfair: public school funding would end up flowing to private school tuition that only the wealthy could afford.

But that is not the case. In a properly implemented voucher system, public schools would be *phased out entirely* and replaced by a wide variety of private schools like those listed below. More importantly, vouchers would also include *apprenticeships* in every field a free-market system has to offer…

SCHOOLS:

Educational choices for classroom or personal learning including but not limited to…

Classical academies
STEM academies
Hybrid homeschool
Online mastery schools
Village-style, one-room schools
Trade academies
Culinary schools
Music conservatories
Homeschool pods
Tech bootcamps
Entrepreneurship labs
Faith-based schools of every type
Montessori microschools
Sports academies
Outdoor survival schools
Arts academies (dance, theater, film)
Etc.

APPRENTICESHIPS:

Apprenticeships from local and online businesses including but not limited to…

Accounting
Biotechnology
Creative & Design
E-commerce
Education
Entertainment
Finance
Healthcare & Medicine
Law
Media
Retail
Service
Trades
Technology
Etc.

With both *private schools for all* and *apprenticeships*, the sky is the limit…

SCHOOL-CHOICE MISCONCEPTION—ONLY EXISTING SCHOOLS:

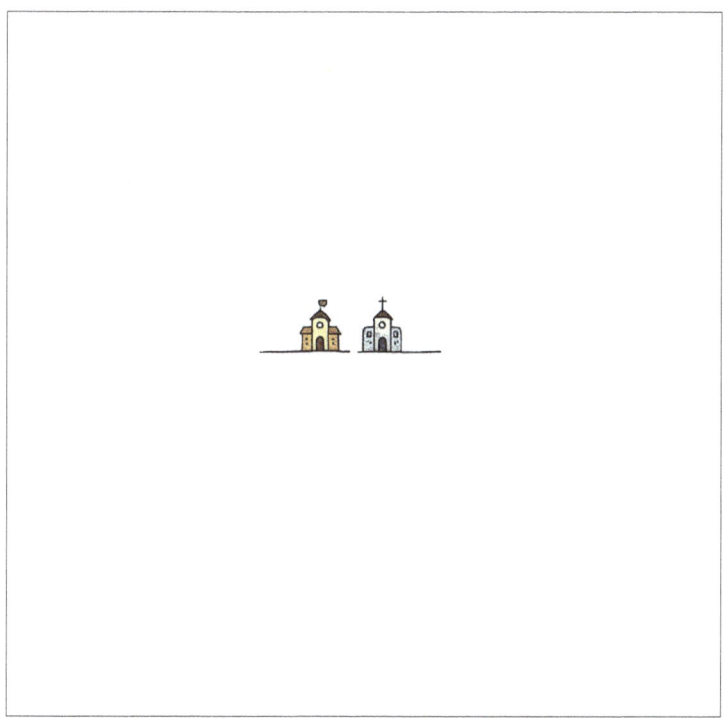

SCHOOL-CHOICE REALITY— A WORLD OF EDUCATIONAL CHOICES:

EXAMPLE FORMULA 2C: WELFARE

This formula can also illustrate how freedom improves lives and the U.S. welfare system is the root of the crime and hopelessness in impoverished communities—whether in Appalachia or the inner cities.

Decades of leftists' deliberate undermining of African American communities: "welfare" for healthy individuals, financial rewards for fatherlessness, and glamorization of crime and drug culture in music, film, and television.

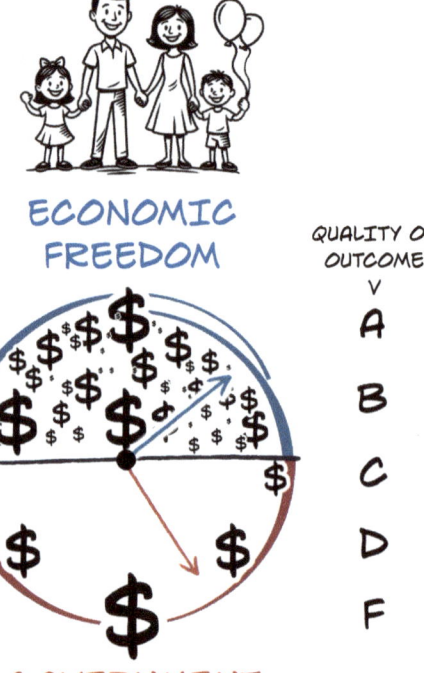

FREEDOM—>

A person in a working family reaches working age, and his or her quality of life (blue compass hand) improves with every good decision. They get a job—bonus!—marry—bonus!—claim their children—bonus!—become a homeowner—bonus!—own a business—bonus!—and enjoy a comfortable retirement with grandkids—bonus!

WELFARE—>

Remember, welfare is a lifeline for many. But government dependency punishes positive life decisions and rewards negative ones. Get a job?—lose welfare. Marry?—welfare is cut. Claim your children?—welfare is cut for parents and children. Want to buy a home?—not possible. Get a business loan?—not possible.

In addition, welfare creates negative incentives and drives their red compass hand even lower. Work under the table?—keep your welfare. "Hustle" or steal?—keep your welfare. Join a drug cartel?—keep your welfare. This often leads to prison or an early death.

"What the welfare system and other kinds of governmental programs are doing is paying people to fail.

In so far as they fail, they receive the money; in so far as they succeed—even to a moderate extent—the money is taken away."—*Thomas Sowell*

DEMARXIFICATION—PAGE 68

One solution would be *grace periods*—

I have lived in and around welfare communities. It is well known in these communities that people on welfare will not take a job if the employer is planning to claim them as an employee, because their welfare will be instantly docked.

Why would someone work at McDonald's when they can get the same reward for doing nothing? Would you?

This has people either not working, working in under-the-table situations, or getting involved in crime—all bad options.

This is a well-known issue faced daily by people on welfare, yet it rarely receives attention in public discourse.

Many individuals, regardless of skin color, will never recover from the damage done by this system. But something must be done to begin to heal these communities and end the cycle of dependency.

People who were put on lifelong welfare deserve grace periods—"reparations" if you will. "Welfare" would no longer instantly punish work. Long-term welfare recipients would be allowed to keep *both* their benefits and a paycheck for a period of time.

After that *grace period*, benefits would be gradually phased out as they transition into productive, lasting careers. Ultimately, the lifelong harm that results from paying healthy people to do nothing could be phased out.

The grace periods would allow welfare recipients to leave the socialist system engineered for failure, and join the rest of Americans in capitalism/economic freedom.

Imagine the day grace periods are implemented, and the yoke of welfare is lifted. For the first time in their lives, recipients wake to the same world of opportunity we take for granted. They can take a *real* job without fearing the loss of the lifeline they've relied on since birth. One act of policy—an entire community is transformed. What a day that would be.

FORMULA 2C—IN SUMMARY:

Consumers have the power—and the numbers—but we've been conditioned to believe we are powerless.

Decade after decade, instead of exerting our power as consumers, we allow bureaucrats to control us—and trillions of our hard-earned dollars. For generations, we've been taught to accept this without question as "democracy."

Even worse, today's students are being taught to demand bureaucrats be given *even more* power in the name of "socialism."

It took generations of warping minds[136] to bring us to this point. Imagine how different the world would be if, for all that time, instead of repetition of socialist slogans, students had been taught that consumers have the power and that millions of Americans surrendering our power to a small number of politicians assures corruption.

School choice is a good place to start, and can be achieved one community at a time.

Voucher systems and apprenticeships are gaining traction nationwide. One leading organization advancing this work is EdChoice.org, founded by Milton Friedman and Rose D. Friedman, which provides education, research, and advocacy on school choice.

Section 3

FORMULA 3A
Weapons of Mass Distraction

FORMULA 3B
Offending the Few vs. Harming Everyone

FORMULA 3C
Spinning Our Wheels—Pros, Cons & Missed Opportunities

FORMULA 3A

Weapons of Mass Distraction

In the past, we were taught to see the media as a watchdog, the "fourth estate," protecting us from government and corporate corruption.[137]

Today, mainstream media—far from being watchdogs—have been weaponized against free people.[138] Together with corrupt authorities and institutions, they employ various tactics to deceive legitimate populations. One such method involves hyperfocusing on "molehills" while disregarding "mountains."

It's a double whammy: while these cherry-picked narratives harm and divide us, major problems, root causes, and solutions also go unaddressed.

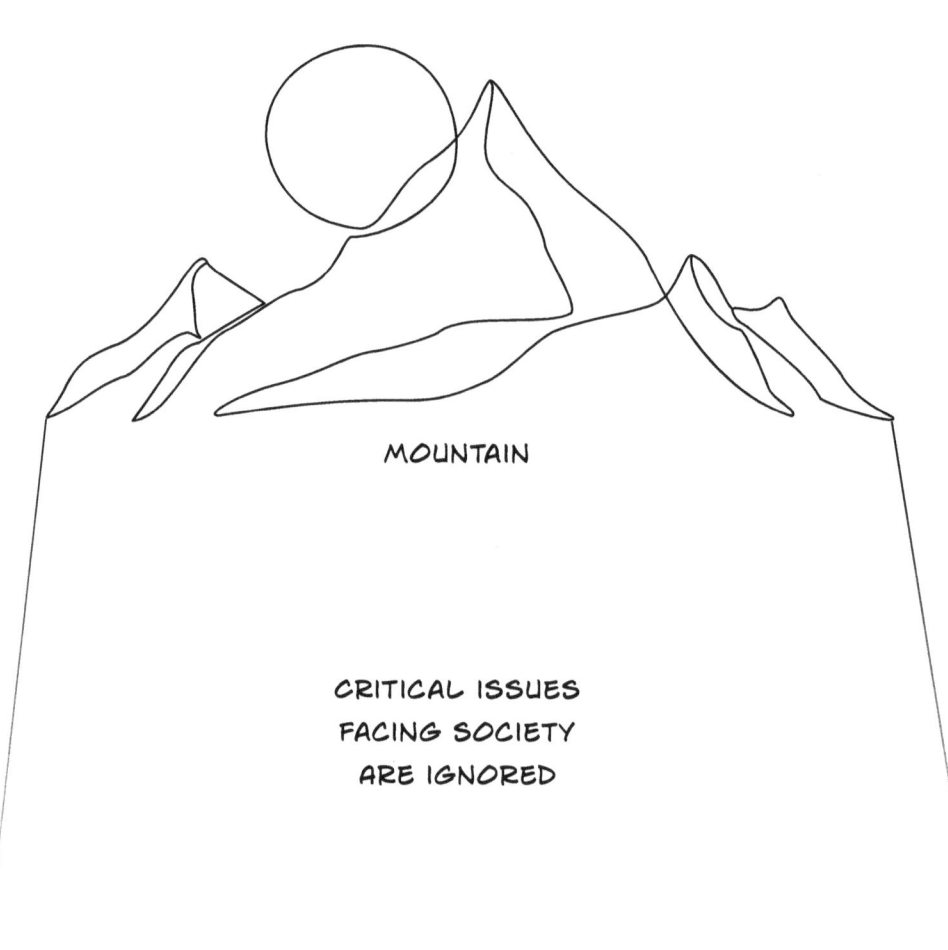

MOUNTAIN

CRITICAL ISSUES FACING SOCIETY ARE IGNORED

MOLEHILL

MEDIA CHERRY-PICKED NARRATIVES ARE HYPERFOCUSED UPON

This simple formula helps distinguish what's cherry-picked from what's critical—and analyze the motives of those promoting each.

EXAMPLE: PROBLEMS IN THE UNITED STATES

We have serious problems facing our country. Our media, academia and other institutions are supposed to be watchdogs but not only do they no longer do their job, they are actively working against the best interests of society.

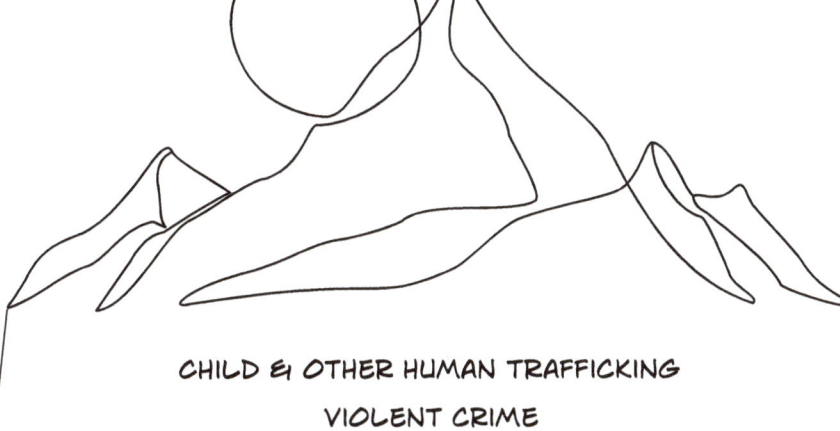

CHILD & OTHER HUMAN TRAFFICKING
VIOLENT CRIME
HOMELESSNESS
DRUG ADDICTION
MASS ILLEGAL IMMIGRATION
GOVERNMENTAL & INSTITUTIONAL CORRUPTION
BROKEN FAMILIES & FATHERLESSNESS
FAILING PUBLIC SCHOOLS
GROCERY STORES WITH MOSTLY UNHEALTHY FOOD
CORRUPTION & COST OF HEALTHCARE
UNEMPLOYMENT
SOCIALIST WELFARE SYSTEM
WEAPONIZATION OF LEGAL SYSTEMS
INFLATION & NATIONAL DEBT
BIG-TECH CENSORSHIP
ETC.

ANY DIVISIVE INDIVIDUAL INCIDENT THAT DIVIDES AMERICANS, VILIFIES LAW ENFORCEMENT, OR DEMONIZES THE MAJORITY POPULATION

EXAMPLE: "CLIMATE CHANGE" ALARMISM

BOGUS CLAIM: 97–99% SCIENTIFIC CONSENSUS[139]

The papers that allege a 97–99% scientific consensus—Cook et al.[140] and Lynas et al.[141]—are anything but scientific. Their own numbers contradict their conclusions. For example, the Lynas study, whose headline claims a "99% consensus," shows in its own data and pie chart that 68.44% of papers actually took *no position* and an additional 15.32% agreement with consensus was "implied."

While we focus on "climate change" as our only environmental threat, real threats are ignored and solutions are not imagined let alone implemented.

ENVIRONMENTAL CONCERNS
LARGELY IGNORED INCLUDE:

AIR AND WATER POLLUTION
DEFORESTATION
DISPOSABLE FASHION
ELECTRONIC WASTE FROM SOLAR PANELS, WIND TURBINES, AND ELECTRIC BATTERIES
ENDANGERED SPECIES
HUMANE TREATMENT OF ANIMALS
LOSS OF BIODIVERSITY AND NATURAL HABITATS
OVERFISHING
POVERTY
RESOURCE DEPLETION
WATER SCARCITY
AND MORE

"CLIMATE CHANGE!"

Today, centralized institutions have far too much power—especially over young people who have not developed the ability to think independently. Teachers are making children lose sleep over "climate change."

Although the vast majority of these teachers believe they are teaching something of value, they are actually grooming children for future submission to global dictates that will eliminate legitimate populations' power and freedoms.

FORMULA 3B

Offending the Few vs. Harming Everyone

The pattern in this formula is frequently observed in the deceptive narratives of our time. It involves either:

Focusing on a minority of negative incidents while denying that the majority of incidents are positive.

Creating the illusion of popular support by amplifying a minority of supporters.[142]

Fixating on historic or rare failures while ignoring massive, ongoing successes.

The focus will be put on a single incident or small group that perpetuates a political agenda.

Problems and solutions facing entire communities are not discussed.

EXAMPLE: GEORGE FLOYD

The death of George Floyd received 24/7, wall-to-wall coverage from the media.

In the same year—2020—6,940 Blacks committed homicide and 6,181 Blacks were murdered,[143] but these tragedies received little national media coverage. Why?

Again, in true Marxist fashion, this formula hurts everyone. Leftist media and NGOs exploited Floyd's tragic death to ignite riots—causing more death, injury, and billions in damage. They stoked hatred toward police and created racial tensions, all while ignoring root issues *entirely*. Solutions to high murder rates go undiscussed and unanswered.

EXAMPLE: PUTTING DOWN THE UNITED STATES

This example is a common misrepresentation of free America.

The statement "America wasn't great for everyone" is of course true, but *completely inane*.
There is no such thing as a country that was "great for everyone."

As a matter of fact, life for the vast majority of human beings prior to the 20th Century was more difficult than any of us can imagine. Many places today still suffer from conditions that the U.S. overcame generations ago.

American media, academia and other institutions will...

1. Focus on some groups who historically suffered from IMPERIALISM in the U.S.

2. Ignore the fact that American CAPITALISM has lifted more people of every race and background out of poverty, expanded rights faster and farther than any other society, and continues to attract millions who risk everything to get in.

Many Americans who grow up surrounded by freedom, abundance, and stability fail to recognize how rare those conditions truly are—especially young people. Deceived by narratives that portray the United States as "racist" and "irredeemably" flawed, some leave in an attempt to prove that the rest of the world is more loving, tolerant, and just—only to be confronted by harsh realities.[144]

FORMULA 3C

Spinning Our Wheels—
Pros, Cons & Missed Opportunities

As illustrated in the previous two formulas, corrupt institutions keep us trapped on a habitrail of divisive, tit-for-tat narratives. Root problems and real solutions are ignored.

The following simple A–B–C comparison helps analyze these situations in detail by encouraging us to make thorough lists that include both the distracting narratives and the underlying root issues and solutions.

These comparison lists can be used in a variety of ways depending on the topic.

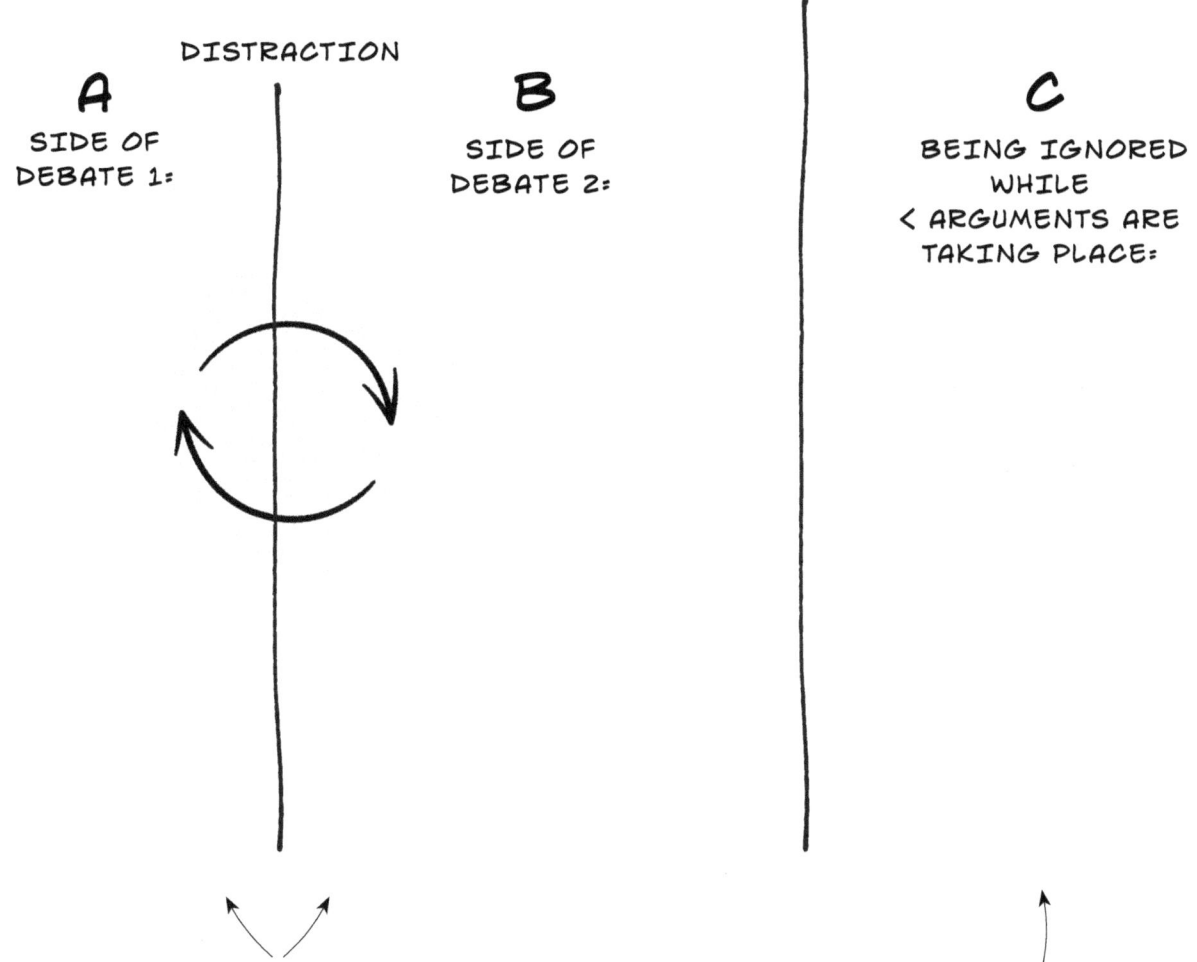

DISTRACTION

A — SIDE OF DEBATE 1:

B — SIDE OF DEBATE 2:

C — BEING IGNORED WHILE ARGUMENTS ARE TAKING PLACE:

Corrupt institutions have us spinning our wheels, debating "**A**" vs. "**B**" on which we have strong opinions.

"**C**" identifies root problems and their solutions—solutions we could all agree on.

But those with institutional power choose to ignore, even suppress, discussion of real problems. Because—for bizarre reasons none of us can relate to—they actually oppose improvement in society.

DEMARXIFICATION—PAGE 78

EXAMPLES: LGBT "PRIDE," "PRO-CHOICE," AND "AFFIRMATIVE ACTION"

A	**B**	**C**
SIDE OF ARGUMENT 1:	SIDE OF ARGUMENT 2:	BEING IGNORED WHILE < ARGUMENTS ARE TAKING PLACE:

LGBT "PRIDE"

A. Celebrating LGBT sexuality in parades, schools, libraries, and other children's venues.

B. Not celebrating LGBT sexuality in parades, schools, libraries, and other children's venues.

C. Teaching kids how to be friends:
- How to be kind and help others.
- How to be a good dad or mom.
- Hard work.
- Critical thinking
- History, math, science, English.
- How to be ladies and gentlemen.
- Home economics.
- Job skills, etc.

"PRO-CHOICE"

A. Meaningless casual sex.

B. The life of an innocent human being.

C. Figuring out why there's a need for so many abortions, what is causing women to believe that casual sex is more important than human life, and what can be done about it.

Helping to educate children and adults on responsibility before intimate relations, traditional lifestyles, what's best for a successful, happy life, etc.

"AFFIRMATIVE ACTION"

A. College admission standards based on skin color.

B. College admission standards based on academic achievement.

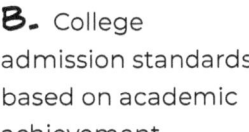

C. Figuring out why some students are not doing as well as others on college admissions. Working to change those root problems—such as poorly performing public schools—and placing students in colleges where they will succeed, etc.

Note: Racial quotas and so-called "affirmative action" imply that certain races require special treatment. Though introduced under the guise of "helping," these policies often set individuals up for avoidable failure by placing them in institutions for which they are academically unprepared. They reinforce racial stereotypes rather than addressing root problems such as failing public schools. As a result, people of color may be unfairly presumed to be diversity hires rather than recognized for their merit.

EXAMPLE: TALL SHIPS CANCELLATION

In 2021, families in Bangor, Maine, were excited to hear that the tall ships were coming to town for a rare spectacle promising fun, history, and education.

Unfortunately, a sponsor of the event, a local bank, was more concerned[145] with political correctness and its ESG score* than with its community. After receiving a letter from a Native American NGO, they forbade a replica of Christopher Columbus's ship—the *Santa Maria*—from participating, which resulted in the cancellation of the entire event in our harbor.

Columbus never set foot on what is now the United States—let alone anywhere near Maine[146]—so what were they actually protesting? The mere presence of Europeans in the Americas?

The simple comparison list on the facing page can outline the pros and cons of situations like this...

As with all Marxist narratives, it was a lose-lose for everyone. The bank's politically correct choice backfired: it caused disappointment, bred hostility, and deprived local citizens and businesses (including Native Americans)—and even the bank itself—of valuable opportunities.

DEMARXIFICATION—PAGE 80

A
HARM FROM CANCELING THE EVENT:

- Families were heartbroken to lose a once-in-a-generation chance to tour the majestic tall ships in our own town. Children missed out on a *living history* that they could not find in a textbook.
- Businesses—even those owned by Native Americans—lost the opportunity to earn substantial additional revenue.
- Local workers—including Native Americans—lost a significant boost to their paychecks.
- Native craftspeople lost out on an opportunity to sell crafts, dreamcatchers, and jewelry to thousands of visitors.
- Far from fostering compassion for Native Americans, this decision bred resentment. The Native group and the bank appeared self-interested and dismissive of their neighbors and community interests.
- Bank customers of European decent were dismayed that their own bank did not defend them when their mere presence in the Americas was deemed offensive.
- The bank's disdain toward European presence, and indifference toward the community's best interests angered many of its customers, causing some to take their banking elsewhere.

B
BENEFITS FROM CANCELING THE EVENT:

C
BROADER ISSUES:

- The focus was on abuses from centuries past, while today's solvable problems in Native American communities were ignored.
- European Americans were cast as villains for nothing more than their heritage.
- Those who wield ESG scores are given a pass while their dictates divide communities.
- The bank's desperate attempt to stay politically correct—despite it hurting everyone, including itself—has made people question its ability to make sound financial decisions.
- This woke decision also erased a rare chance for education and raised awareness on both sides. Bangor Native Americans lost the chance to present their side, and European Americans lost the chance to defend Columbus, who is being unfairly demonized.[148]
- Peaceful education and conversation could have built respect. Instead—thanks to fear of being labeled "politically incorrect"—division and race-based hate won the day.

DOUBLE STANDARDS ARE IN PLAY.

As stated earlier, LGBT individuals are considered "oppressed," and are shielded from criticism. Corrupt institutions exploit this by encouraging well-meaning individuals to hold LGBT events with the children's motifs discussed on page 52, Example 2.

Conversely, European Americans are unfairly labeled as "oppressors," which allows woke institutions to cancel events based on their history without hesitation. They are denied the opportunity to host a wholesome, educational day focused on history and nautical traditions.

Another Maine town welcomed the tall ships, and a protest was indeed held. However, based on media coverage, only a handful of Native Americans attended, along with roughly thirty-five white activists from a local LGBT group. This calls into question claims of widespread Indigenous opposition.

*ESG—"Environmental, Social, and Governance"—is a rating system for businesses that judges behavior and activities, rewarding compliance with the desired norms of those in power—political correctness—and punishing dissent. ESG strips power from consumers and transfers it to unelected individuals with an agenda.[147]

Section 4

ANCILLARY FORMULAS
Countering Marxist Debate Tactics

HOW THE FORMULAS WORK TOGETHER
The Full Demarxification Matrix

SOME SOLUTIONS

REFERENCE ENDNOTES

ANCILLARY FORMULAS

Countering Marxist Debate Tactics

Since leftism seeks to invert reality and cause harm, its positions are difficult, if not impossible, to defend using factual arguments. Some tactics used by neo-Marxists can be called out by referring to these ancillary formulas.

1. PERFECTION/UTOPIAN FALLACY

2. PRESENTISM FALLACY

3. THE STRAW-MAN

4. THE RED HERRING

5. T-SHIRT TEST

6. DEATHBED TEST

7. DEMANDING RIGHTS & CONDITIONS YOU ALREADY POSSESS.

8. GUILTY OF WHAT YOU ACCUSE OTHERS

9. PRIVATE ENTERPRISE VS. GOVERNMENT

PRIVATE ENTERPRISE = SUCCESS!

GOVERNMENT-RUN = FAILURE.

11. DETERMINING GOOD & BAD

10. SLOPE OF DEFENDING WRONG

- LEGITIMATE ARGUMENTS
  - ARGUING EXCEPTIONS
    - INVOKING "EXPERTS"
    - CLAIMING "EXPERTISE"
    - CITING EXCUSES
    - QUESTIONING RELEVANCY
    - OBFUSCATION
    - FILIBUSTERING/TALKING OVER
    - "AGREE TO DISAGREE"
    - ATTACK ASSOCIATIONS
    - AD HOMINEM ATTACKS
    - NAME-CALLING
    - DEMONIZATION
    - WEAPONIZED VICTIMHOOD
    - CENSORING
    - SHOUTING DOWN
    - SILENCING
    - THREATS
    - PROSECUTION
    - VIOLENCE

12. TOP MARXIST TARGETS:

FAMILIES, FARMS & LEGITIMATE BUSINESSES

13. ANYTHING THE WEALTHY CAN HAVE PRIVATELY, EVERYONE CAN HAVE PRIVATELY.

14. MAKING BAD IDEAS SOUND GOOD

1. PERFECTION / UTOPIAN FALLACY
The perfection, or "utopian," fallacy unfairly discredits progress by comparing it to an impossible ideal.

2. PRESENTISM FALLACY
Unfairly judging individuals from centuries ago by today's values.

3. STRAW MAN ARGUMENT
Restates the opponent's view in a weaker version, then attacks that version.

4. RED HERRING
Introduces irrelevant topics to distract from the issue.

5. T-SHIRT TEST
If your group is demeaned or restricted in showing pride in your heritage or skin color, your group is being targeted for vilification—and potentially for retribution.

6. DEATHBED TEST
Picture yourself at life's end. What actions would make you proud, ashamed, or seem meaningless? Let this guide your behavior.

7. DEMANDING CONDITIONS YOU ALREADY HAVE
When people demand rights or conditions they already possess, often without being able to articulate what is lacking.

8. GUILTY OF WHAT YOU ACCUSE OTHERS
Marxism often makes its proponents guilty of the very wrongdoing they accuse others of committing.

9. PRIVATE ENTERPRISE VS. GOVERNMENT
If you want something to succeed, put it in the hands of free enterprise; if you want something to fail, put it in the hands of government.

10. SLOPE OF DEFENDING WRONG
Neo-Marxist arguments, being "post-truth," must quickly descend into increasingly irrational defenses.

11. DETERMINING GOOD & BAD
Ask whether something makes life happier, healthier, and easier—or less happy, less healthy, and more difficult.

12. TOP MARXIST TARGETS
Neo-Marxists target structures that obstruct centralized power: strong families, independent farms, and small businesses.

13. ANYTHING THE WEALTHY CAN HAVE PRIVATELY
Anything the wealthy enjoy privately can be made accessible to everyone through privatization mechanisms like vouchers.

14. MAKING BAD IDEAS SOUND GOOD
Marxism frequently disguises harmful ideas in pleasant-sounding euphemisms.

EXAMPLES: SOME SELECTED EXAMPLES FROM THE PREVIOUS TWO PAGES.

PERFECTION/UTOPIAN FALLACY

"America wasn't great for everyone."

(Inane—no country is or was "great for everyone.")

PRESENTISM FALLACY

Tearing down statues of historical figures because they don't meet today's moral standards erases context and history.

T-SHIRT TEST

Straights, Whites, and men are forbidden from having group-pride organizations, while gays, Blacks, and women are not.

Jews in Nazi Germany were forbidden from gathering; Germans were not.

DEATHBED TEST

A night out partying vs. spending time with your grandma—which one will matter more on that last day?

DEMANDING RIGHTS & CONDITIONS YOU ALREADY POSSESS.

Demanding women's or LGBT rights without being able to name which rights they do not have.

GUILTY OF WHAT YOU ACCUSE OTHERS

Saying "all white people are racist" is racism.

Demanding everyone else take part in gender fantasy or be labeled "fascists" is fascism.

DEI (Diversity, Equity & Inclusion) is the opposite of its claims—judging people by *skin color* rather than the content of their character,[149] forcing unfair *"equity,"* and *excluding* anyone who disagrees.

SLOPE OF DEFENDING WRONG
- LEGITIMATE ARGUMENTS
  - ARGUING EXCEPTIONS
    - INVOKING "EXPERTS"
      - CLAIMING "EXPERTISE"
        - ETC.

Citing rape as a reason for unrestricted abortion access, despite rape exceptions existing in all 50 states.

MAKING BAD IDEAS SOUND GOOD

"Minor-attracted person," "gender-affirming care," "reproductive rights," "healthcare should be a right, not a privilege (see facing page)."

TOP MARXIST TARGETS:

Demonizing traditional family values.

Scaring youth out of having children with climate-catastrophe claims.[150]

Crushing small farms and businesses with regulations only mega-corporations can endure.

DEMARXIFICATION—PAGE 86

MISNOMERS:

Marxists often label entities in a way that is either intentionally softening, blatantly deceptive, or contradictory to their actual purpose. Here are just some:

- "Affirmative Action"
- "Affordable Care Act"
- "Arab Spring"
- "Black Lives Matter"
- "Body Positivity"
- "Citizens United"
- "Denier (climate, election, vaccine) allusion to 'Holocaust denier'"
- "Diversity is a Strength"
- "Diversity, Equity & Inclusion"
- "Environmental, Social & Governance."
- "Feeding Our Future"
- "Federal Reserve"
- "Feminist"
- "Fiscal Responsibilities Act"
- "Food Action Alliance"
- "Food Innovation Hubs"
- "Gay Pride"
- "Gender Affirming Surgery"
- "Global Food Security"
- "Globalism"
- "Great Leap Forward"
- "Healthcare is a Right, Not a Privilege"
- "Human Trafficking"
- "Inclusive"
- "Intelligence Agencies"
- "Love is Love"
- "Minor-Attracted Person"
- "My Body, My Choice"
- "National Childhood Vaccine Injury Act of 1986"
- "Net Neutrality"
- "Open Borders"
- "Open Society"
- "Party for Neighborly Love, Freedom & Diversity"
- "Patriot Act"
- "People's Liberation Army"
- "Planned Parenthood"
- "Pro-Choice"
- "Public Healthcare"
- "Reparations"
- "Reproductive Justice"
- "Sex Positive"
- "Social Justice"
- "Socialism"
- "Special Interests"
- "Sustainable Development"
- "The Cares Act"
- "The Greater Good"
- "Unions"
- "United Nations"
- "Universal Basic Income"
- "War on Drugs"
- "Wealth Redistribution"
- "Welfare Benefits"
- "Well-Camp (Aussie)"
- "Women's Health Protection Act"
- "World Health Organization"
- "Etc."

Former President Barack Obama, Senator Bernie Sanders, and many individuals on the left argue that healthcare should be a "right, not a privilege." This sounds lovely, correct? We all want people to be healthy and have access to healthcare. However, it's actually quite evil...

What gives you the "right" to the labor of healthcare workers?

Healthcare workers have difficult jobs, expensive educations, and deserve to be paid well. Consider Yeonmi Park's accounts of healthcare workers in North Korea who earn $1-$2 a month.[151] What kind of people believe they have the "right to the labor of others?" Slave owners do. Communist dictators do. So, with some critical thought, Obama's and Sanders' "good sounding" sentiment can be likened to forced labor.

SUMMARY

How the Formulas Work Together

This matrix can be applied in the discussion of virtually any topic while maintaining a focus on truth, freedom, and traditional values. At the same time, it exposes the nefarious patterns of leftist manipulation.

EXAMPLE: SOCIETAL SUBVERSION

1. We vote for surrogate decision-makers...
2. who will fall somewhere on the stairway to corruption.
3. Those who are corrupt...
4. wish to manipulate free populations.
5. They will employ corrupt institutions to hyperfocus on cherry-picked narratives...
6. that will divide free people into "oppressed" and "oppressors."
7. This harms both groups involved...
8. while ignoring actual problems that require solutions.
9. Creating hatred of traditionally beneficial entities and actions like law enforcement, traditional families, hard work, and anyone they perceive as a threat...
10. and tolerating destructive behavior like crime, casual sex, and drug use...
11. based on the belief that good and bad are "relative."
12. Those in power who claim to oppose relativism do so weakly...
13. and spin their wheels by engaging in divisive "tit-for-tat"...
14. while true solutions are ignored.

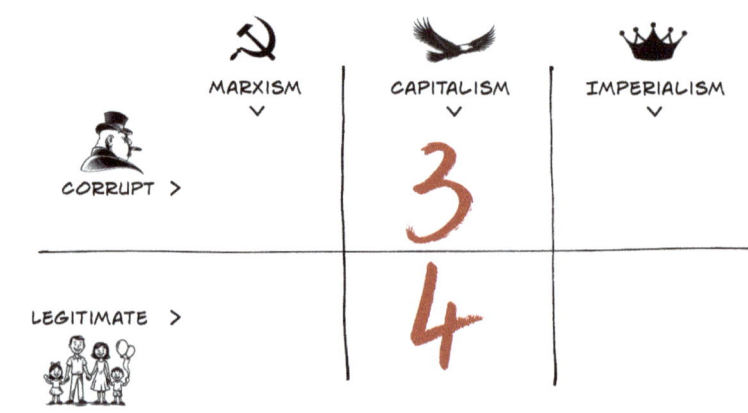

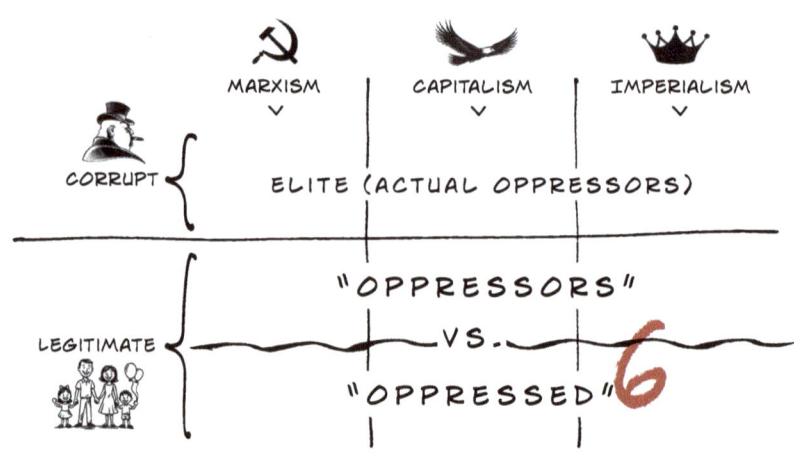

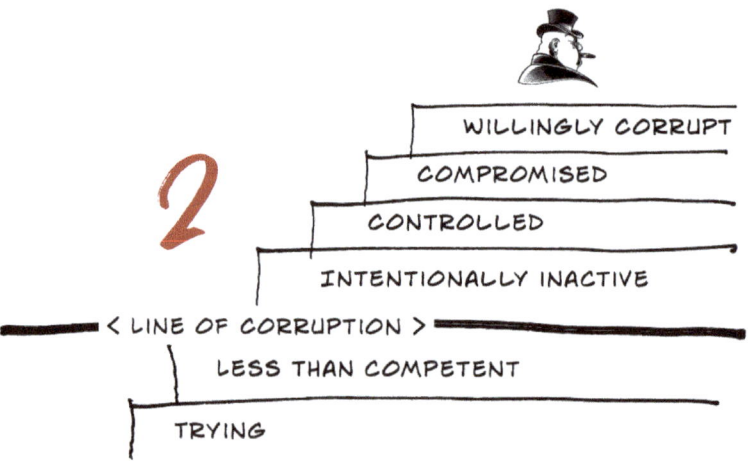

DEMARXIFICATION—PAGE 88

For space reasons I have not included the ancillary formulas, but they are essential for debate. Simply place the formulas from page 84 to the right of this page.

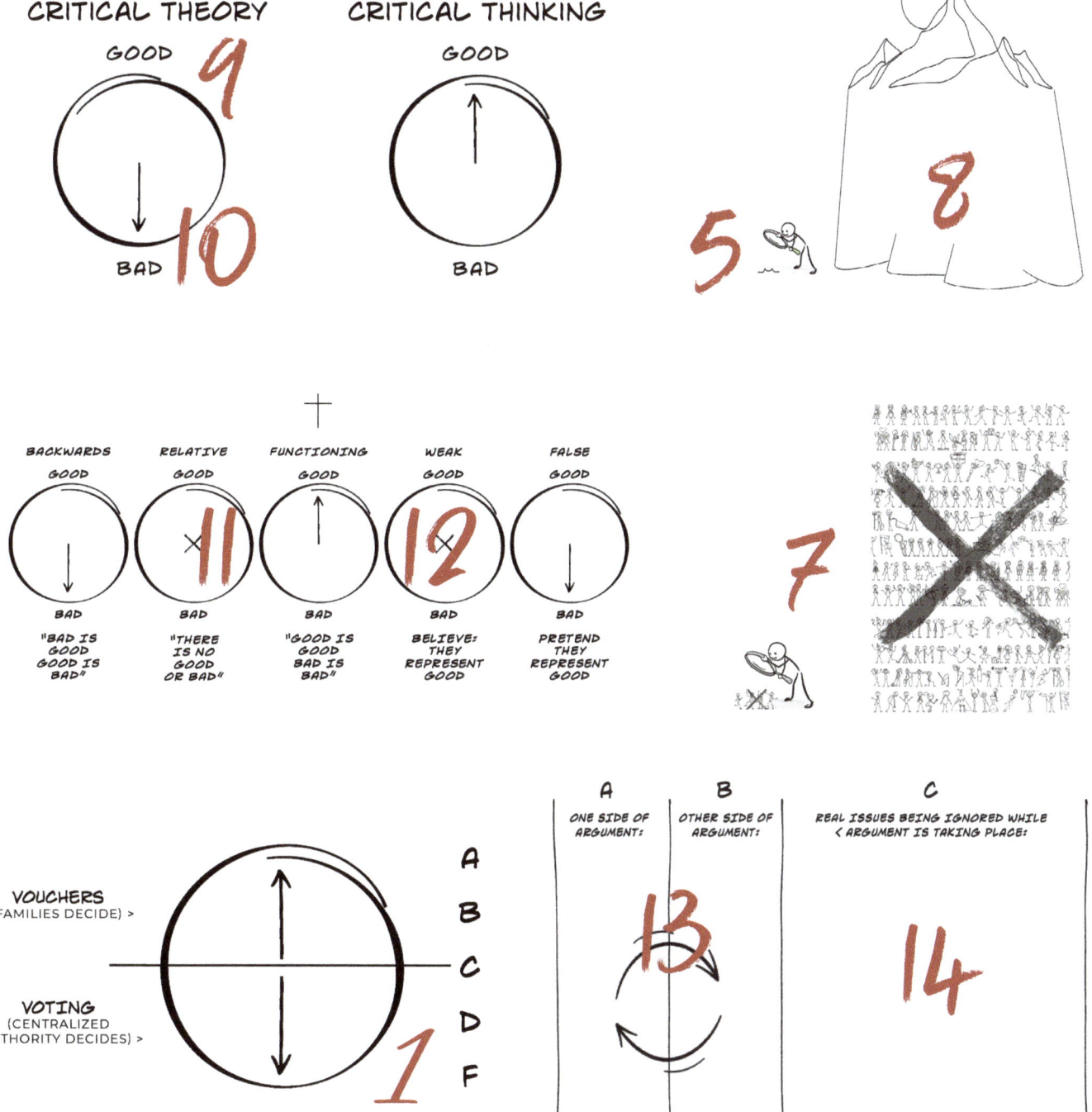

For practical demonstrations of the formulas and the discussion matrix, visit DEMARXIFICATION.COM. There, you can view free videos and download a file of the complete matrix.

Some Solutions:

Most institutions today are opposed to society's improvement, so it is important that we begin developing our own solutions. Here are just a few:

1. Envision true economic freedom (ideal capitalism) and begin formulating strategies to work toward it. See Formulas 1A, page 12, and 2C, page 62.

2. Stop allowing the word *capitalism* (economic freedom) to be demonized. Freedom is always good. See Formula 1A, page 12.

3. Note that capitalism achieves what Marxism claims to want: power to workers and regulation of businesses through consumer choice. See Formula 1A, page 12.

4. Reject narratives that divide populations by painting groups of people as "oppressed" or "oppressors." See Formula 1B, page 26.

5. Acknowledge that corrupt leaders who seek to divide us are the true enemy—and that our allies should be one another. See Formulas 1B, page 26; 2A, page 38; and 3B, page 75.

6. It's not Russia vs. Ukraine, Israel vs. Palestine, or *Hutus* vs. *Tutsis*—it's corrupt centralized authorities vs. world populations. See Formula 1B, page 26.

7. Assess authorities and institutions to determine their level of corruption or legitimacy. See Formula 1C, page 34.

8. Stop blaming one group for the conditions of another, and instead, solve problems using critical thought: facts, truth, experience, and objective reality. See Formula 2A, page 38.

9. Make wholesome cool, and push back against the glorification of bad behavior by Hollywood and other powerful institutions. See Formula 2A, page 38.

10. Teach young people to embrace honesty: *Am I wrong? Could my professors—or the media—be wrong?* And to consider evidence objectively. See Formula 2A, page 38.

11. Teach young men and women how wonderful traditional gender roles are, and that modern "feminism" is far from feminine. See Formula 2A examples, page 38.

12. Recognize that good and bad are not relative and that relativism is a deceptive tactic used to justify destructive behavior. See Formula 2B, page 50.

13. Not everyone who says they are a Christian is actually Christian. See Formula 2B, page 50.

14. Imagine ways to peacefully shift decision-making from centralized authorities to individuals and families. See Formula 2C, page 62.

15. Limit the power of centralized authorities to the original American ideal: determining the will of the people and ensuring its implementation. See Formula 2C, page 62.

16. Reimagine our educational systems and return to teaching young people through apprenticeships—with the whole community contributing to education. See Formula 2C, page 62.

17. Force colleges to compete with the real world. See Formula 2C, page 62.

18. Stop blaming skin color for the problems in impoverished neighborhoods. Implement grace periods or other reforms to end the destructive impact of the U.S. welfare system on communities. See Formula 2C, page 62.

19. Privatize institutions so that power is shifted from bureaucrats to taxpayers, and families have choices from a variety of free-market entities who compete for taxpayer vouchers. See Formula 2C, page 62.

20. Focus on critical issues and reject institutions that distract us with the "outrage of the week." See Formula 3A, page 72.

21. Ask what kind of people promote harmful narratives like "transgender children" while ignoring child sex trafficking—and whether these are trustworthy sources of information. See Formula 3A, page 72.

22. Recognize and reject entities that promote divisive narratives. See Formula 3B, page 75.

23. Notice when minorities are being exploited as a tool to harm both them and the broader population. See Formula 3B, page 75.

24. Acknowledge that we like each other, that our differences are beautiful, and that we're fascinated by one another's cultures.[152] See Formula 3B, page 75.

25. Get off the *Habitrail* of corrupt media's endless tit-for-tat narratives. Start envisioning real solutions to society's root problems. See Formula 3C, page 77.

26. Educate students to avoid misleading arguments and to stay focused on actual topics. See the Ancillary Formulas, page 84.

Learn the simple way to defeat indoctrination.

Reserve Lisa Rahon, the creator of *DeMarxification*, for a live presentation or webinar tailored to your classroom, event, or meeting.

Email info@demarxification.com for information & booking.

Endnotes

1. Union Films, "The Communist Takeover Explained (1966)," YouTube video, 7:35, October 23, 2022, https://www.youtube.com/watch?v=I7zNy4gfx8U

2. Jordan B. Peterson, "The Wounds That Won't Heal | Detransitioner Chloe Cole | EP 319," YouTube video, 2:01:36, January 2, 2023, https://youtu.be/6O3MzPeomqs

3. U.S. Declaration of Independence, July 4, 1776, National Archives, https://www.archives.gov/founding-docs/declaration

4. Russell Freedman, *The Boston Tea Party*, illus. by Peter Malone (New York: Holiday House, 2013)

5. Gavin Weightman, *The Industrial Revolutionaries: The Making of the Modern World, 1776–1914* (New York: Grove Press, 2007).

6. Wolfgang Schivelbusch, *The Railway Journey: The Industrialization of Time and Space in the 19th Century* (Berkeley: University of California Press, 2014).

7. *Downton Abbey* (TV series), created by Julian Fellowes, Carnival Films, 2010–2015.

8. David Cannadine, *The Decline and Fall of the British Aristocracy* (New Haven: Yale University Press, 1990), 323–41; Anne de Courcy, *The Husband Hunters: Social Climbing in London and New York* (New York: St. Martin's Press, 2018), 15–20.

9. Anthony B. Kim and Terry Miller, *2023 Index of Economic Freedom* (Washington, DC: The Heritage Foundation, 2023).

10. Roy Beck, "World Poverty, Immigration and Gumballs," video, NumbersUSA, 2010, 6:47, https://www.youtube.com/watch?v=LPjzfGChGIE

11. RAND Corporation, "Gun Ownership in America," Gun Policy in America, accessed September 17, 2025, https://www.rand.org/research/gun-policy/gun-ownership.html

12. Joshua Philipp, *The Dark Origins of Communism,* documentary series, 1 season, hosted by Joshua Philipp, *The Epoch Times,* 2021, HD, https://subscribe.theepochtimes.com/p/?page=originsofcommunism

13. Dennis Prager, "Are Leftists and Liberals Different? | Master's Program," PragerU, YouTube video, 36:15, December 14, 2025, https://www.youtube.com/watch?v=QP9thfJ41rA&t=2048s

14. Karl Marx and Friedrich Engels, *The Communist Manifesto* (New York: Race Point Publishing, 2014).

15. Karl Marx, *Das Kapital: A Critique of Political Economy*, trans. Ben Fowkes (London: Penguin Classics, 1990).

16. George Orwell, *1984* (New York: Signet Classics, 1977).

17. Marx and Engels, *The Communist Manifesto*

18. The White House, *Build Back Better Framework,* August 13, 2025, White House Archives, https://bidenwhitehouse.archives.gov/build-back-better/

19. Marx and Engels, *The Communist Manifesto*

20. Orwell, *1984*.

21. Stéphane Courtois, Nicolas Werth, Jean-Louis Panné, Andrzej Paczkowski, Karel Bartosek, and Jean-Louis Margolin, *The Black Book of Communism: Crimes, Terror, Repression*, trans. Jonathan Murphy and Mark Kramer (Cambridge, MA: Harvard University Press, 1999).

22. Zheng Yi, *Scarlet Memorial: Tales of Cannibalism in Modern China,* trans. T. P. Sym (Boulder, CO: Westview Press, 1996); Yan Lianke, *Marrow,* trans. Carlos Rojas (New York: Grove Press, 2017).

23. Alvaro Vargas Llosa, "Venezuela and the Road to Serfdom," *Independent Institute,* February 14, 2019, https://www.independent.org/news/article.asp?id=10455

24. Jordan B. Peterson, "#1070 – Jordan Peterson," *The Joe Rogan Experience,* PowerfulJRE, streamed live January 30, 2018, video, 2:28:52, at 39:07, https://www.youtube.com/watch?v=6T-7pUEZfgdI; and Thomas Sowell, "The Quest for Cosmic Justice," Hoover Institution, n.d., accessed October 14, 2025, https://www.hoover.org/research/quest-cosmic-justice

25. Yeonmi Park with Maryanne Vollers, *In Order to Live: A North Korean Girl's Journey to Freedom* (New York: Penguin Press, 2015).

26. Jordan B. Peterson, "Tyranny, Slavery and Columbia U | Yeonmi Park | EP 172," *The Jordan B. Peterson Podcast,* YouTube video, 1:34:07, June 27, 2022, https://www.youtube.com/watch?v=8y-qa-SdJtT4; Yeonmi Park, *While Time Remains: A North Korean Defector's Search for Freedom in America* (New York: Portfolio/Penguin, 2023)

27. Thomas J. DiLorenzo, "How Universities Silence Truth—And What We Can Do About It," Mises Media, October 8, 2015, 35:24, YouTube video, https://www.youtube.com/watch?v=JS3ttzqTBqA

28. Christopher F. Rufo, "The Long March Through the Institutions" | Ep. 2, YouTube video, 43:52, June 6, 2024, https://youtu.be/NEt9XepeGt4?si=e8z5SMV_URmGoYfZ; Rudi Dutschke, quoted in Richard Gombin, *The Origins of Modern Leftism* (London: Penguin Books, 1975)

29. The Last Western Man, "The Architects of Western Decline: The Frankfurt School," YouTube video, June 27, 2022, 1:23:45, https://www.youtube.com/watch?v=3JPNhyn-xIs

30. Ruqayyah Darby Hamid and Eric J. Schisgall, "More than Three-Quarters of Surveyed Harvard Faculty Identify as Liberal," *The Harvard Crimson,* May 22, 2023, https://www.thecrimson.com/article/2023/5/22/faculty-survey-2023-politics/

31. Michael Chapman, "Young Americans Like Socialism Too Much—That's a Problem Libertarians Must Fix," *Cato Institute,* May 15, 2025, 1:37 p.m., https://www.cato.org/blog/young-americans-socialism-problem-libertarians-must-fix

32. Patrisse Cullors, interview by Jared Ball, *The Real News Network,* July 2015, https://therealnews.com

33. Rory Carroll, "Sean Penn Praises Chávez as 'Charismatic,'" *The Guardian,* March 6, 2013, https://www.theguardian.com/world/2013/mar/06/sean-penn-hugo-chavez

34. Heather Mac Donald, "Are the Police Racist? | 5 Minute Video," PragerU, YouTube video, 5:11, August 22, 2016, https://www.youtube.com/watch?v=UQCQFH5wOJo; Heather Mac Donald, *The War on Cops: How the New Attack on Law and Order Makes Everyone Less Safe* (New York: Encounter Books, 2016).

35. Ángela Martínez-Monteagudo, María Carmen Martínez-Monteagudo, and Beatriz Delgado, "School Bullying and Cyberbullying in Academically Gifted Students: A Systematic Review," *Aggression and Violent Behavior* 71 (July–August 2023): article 101842, https://doi.org/10.1016/j.avb.2023.101842.

36. Irving L. Janis, *Victims of Groupthink: A Psychological Study of Foreign-Policy Decisions and Fiascoes* (Boston: Houghton Mifflin, 1972).

37. Douglas Murray, *The War on the West* (New York: HarperCollins, 2022); and Douglas Murray, "Why the West Must Defend Itself," *PragerU,* YouTube video, 5:03, February 9, 2022, https://www.youtube.com/watch?v=jUFC6Z5n_pE.

38. Dave Rubin, "Why I Left the Left." Video, 4:22, Produced by PragerU, February 6, 2017. https://youtu.be/hiVQ8vrGA_8

39. American Advocates, "20 Minute Compilation of Liberals CELEBRATING The Death of Charlie Kirk," YouTube video, 26:40, September 13, 2025, https://www.youtube.com/watch?v=_Xa1gO4dWg0

40. Turning Point USA, YouTube channel, accessed October 15, 2025, https://www.youtube.com/@turningpointusa

41. Sky News Australia, "Lefties Losing It: The left is celebrating Charlie Kirk's murder," YouTube video, 15:23, September 11, 2025, https://www.youtube.com/watch?v=dy3f4FFwgPU

42. Daniel Jonah Goldhagen, *Hitler's Willing Executioners: Ordinary Germans and the Holocaust* (New York: Alfred A. Knopf, 1996); and Christopher R. Browning, *Ordinary Men: Reserve*

Police Battalion 101 and the Final Solution in Poland (New York: HarperCollins, 1992).

43 Frank Dikötter, *The Cultural Revolution: A People's History, 1962–1976* (New York: Bloomsbury, 2016); and Jung Chang, *Wild Swans: Three Daughters of China* (New York: Anchor Books, 1991).

44 Yuri Bezmenov (Official Channel), "Yuri Bezmenov Official Channel," YouTube, accessed September 22, 2025, https://www.youtube.com/@bezmenov/videos

45 Yuri Bezmenov, interview by G. Edward Griffin, *Soviet Subversion of the Free-World Press: An Interview with Yuri Bezmenov (1984),* YouTube video, 1:21:05, June 12, 2013, https://www.youtube.com/watch?v=y3qkf3bajd4

46 Orwell, *1984.*

47 Vladimir I. Lenin, *Imperialism: The Highest Stage of Capitalism,* trans. Jos. Fineberg (New York: International Publishers, 1939)

48 Aleksandr Solzhenitsyn, *The Gulag Archipelago, 1918–1956: An Experiment in Literary Investigation,* trans. Thomas P. Whitney (New York: Harper & Row, 1974).

49 Whitney Alyse Webb, *One Nation Under Blackmail: The Sordid Union Between Intelligence and Crime that Gave Rise to Jeffrey Epstein,* vols. 1–2 (Baton Rouge, LA: TrineDay, 2022–2023).

50 Yeonmi Park, "Yeonmi Park at Hannibal-LaGrange University," Free Society, YouTube video, April 27, 2023, 1:12:11, quote at 44:16, https://www.youtube.com/watch?v=wFgrSSvJEg0; Yeonmi Park, *While Time Remains: A North Korean Defector's Search for Freedom in America* (New York: Portfolio/Penguin, 2023).

51 Howard Zinn, *A People's History of the United States* (New York: Harper & Row, 1980).

52 Nikole Hannah-Jones, Caitlin Roper, Ilena Silverman, and Jake Silverstein, eds., *The 1619 Project: A New Origin Story* (New York: Random House, 2021).

53 Vladimir Lenin, *Imperialism: The Highest Stage of Capitalism* (Peking: Foreign Languages Press, 1970).

54 Agnieszka Holland, *Mr. Jones* (Warsaw: Film Produkcja / WestEnd Films, 2019), feature film depicting the Soviet-engineered famine in Ukraine and the excesses of the Communist Party elite..

55 Dambisa Moyo, "Africa with Dambisa Moyo," Hoover Institution, YouTube video, June 23, 2009, https://www.youtube.com/watch?v=eF6y-DIZas68&t=542s; Dambisa Moyo, *Dead Aid: Why Aid Is Not Working and How There Is a Better Way for Africa* (New York: Farrar, Straus and Giroux, 2009).

56 Richard Pipes, *The Bolshevik Revolution* (New York: Alfred A. Knopf, 1990); Anne Applebaum, *Red Famine: Stalin's War on Ukraine* (New York: Doubleday, 2017); Aleksandr Solzhenitsyn, *The Gulag Archipelago, 1918–1956,* trans. Thomas P. Whitney (New York: Harper & Row, 1973).

57 Peterson-KFF, "How Does Health Spending in the U.S. Compare to Other Countries?," *Health System Tracker,* April 9, 2025.

58 LiveNOW from FOX. "WATCH FULL: RFK Jr. hosts American Health Crisis Roundtable with doctors and nutritionists," YouTube video, September 23, 2024. https://www.youtube.com/watch?v=2iWE465RCOk.

59 Janice Hopkins Tanne, "Financial Ties Common between U.S. Medical Schools and Drug Companies," *British Medical Journal* (2007).

60 Tucker Carlson, "Calley Means & Casey Means: How Big Pharma Keeps You Sick, and the Dark Truth About Ozempic and the Pill," *The Tucker Carlson Show*, video, 2:20:56, August 16, 2024.

61 Ben Carson, "Neuralink, God's Hand in Neuroscience and Human Consciousness" (SRS #183), *Shawn Ryan Show,* YouTube video, March 17, 2025, 2:17:42, at 0:04:00.

62 United States. *National Childhood Vaccine Injury Act of 1986,* Pub. L. 99-660, 100 Stat. 3755 (November 14, 1986).

63 Marina Watts, "In Smithsonian Race Guidelines, Rational Thinking and Hard Work Are White Values," *Newsweek*, July 17, 2020, https://www.newsweek.com/smithsonian-race-guidelines-rational-thinking-hard-work-are-white-values-1518333

64 Magatte Wade, "Africa, Capitalism, Communism, and the Future of Humanity (Lex Fridman Podcast #311, August 13, 2022)," YouTube video, https://www.youtube.com/watch?v=Q6tDV3BhrcM; Magatte Wade, *The Heart of a Cheetah: How We Have Been Lied to about African Poverty, and What That Means for Human Flourishing* (Lexington, KY: Cheetah Press, 2023).

65 Dinesh D'Souza, *Death of a Nation: Plantation Politics and the Making of the Democratic Party* (Washington, DC: Regnery Publishing, 2018).

66 Howard Zinn, *A People's History of the United States, 1492–Present* (New York: Harper & Row, 1980); and Nikole Hannah-Jones et al., *The 1619 Project: A New Origin Story* (New York: One World, 2021).

67 Thomas Sowell, *A Conflict of Visions: Ideological Origins of Political Struggles* (New York: Basic Books, 2007); and Thomas Sowell, *Discrimination and Disparities* (New York: Basic Books, 2018).

68 Eric Kaufmann, "How They LIED for 60 Years—Eric Kaufmann Exposes the Progressive Myth (#44)," *Beyond Gender,* YouTube video, October 23, 2025, https://www.youtube.com/watch?v=ufHgZK9QFI4; Eric Kaufmann, profile page, Manhattan Institute, https://manhattan.institute/person/eric-kaufmann.

69 Dr. Jordan B. Peterson and Eric Kaufmann, "Women, Politics, Personality, and Self Esteem | Eric Kaufmann | EP 453," YouTube video, June 6, 2024, 1:54:22, https://www.youtube.com/watch?v=xyOSjWiVBFA

70 Jordan B. Peterson, "Irreversible Damage? | Abigail Shrier | EP 159," YouTube video, March 22, 2021, 1:32:04, https://www.youtube.com/watch?v=fSKQfATa-1I

71 Jordan B. Peterson, "Trans Worship and Child Sacrifice: The New Paganism | Dr. Jared Ross | EP 494," YouTube video, 1:15:53, October 31, 2024, posted by Jordan B. Peterson, https://www.youtube.com/watch?v=vvCv2Ei8fR4&t=171s

72 "GOTTA TEACH THE KIDS" (@thejeffreymarsh), "Untitled YouTube Short," YouTube video, November 17, 2022, https://youtube.com/shorts/6uE_q6J6Rg4

73 Jordan B. Peterson, "Irreversible Damage at Fourteen | Detransitioner Clementine Breen," The Jordan B. Peterson Podcast, March 20, 2025, 1:40:30, YouTube video, https://www.youtube.com/watch?v=IKljKfHNOzw

74 Grand View Research, *U.S. Sex Reassignment Surgery Market Size, Share & Trends Analysis Report By Gender Transition (Female-to-male, Male-to-female), By Procedure (Mastectomy, Vaginoplasty, Scrotoplasty, Hysterectomy, Phalloplasty), And Segment Forecasts, 2023–2030* (San Francisco: Grand View Research, 2025), accessed December 12, 2025, https://www.grandviewresearch.com/industry-analysis/us-sex-reassignment-surgery-market

75 Jordan B. Peterson, "The Wounds That Won't Heal | Detransitioner Chloe Cole | EP 319," YouTube video, 2:01:36, January 2, 2023, https://youtu.be/6O3MzPeomqs

76 Yeonmi Park, interviewed by Nick Shirley, "North Korean Escapee: How Socialism Brainwashes and Destroys Everything," YouTube video, November 26, 2025, https://youtu.be/r5ipSu_T3ak

77 Matt Walsh. *What Is a Woman?* Directed by Justin Folk. Nashville, TN: The Daily Wire, 2022. Documentary film.

78 Dr. Ben Carson, "Ben Carson: There Is a War on the American Family," YouTube video, 51:00, *American Thought Leaders* (Epoch Times), July 27, 2024, https://www.youtube.com/watch?v=_X34bX7P-2E; Ben Carson with Candy Carson, *The Perilous Fight: Overcoming Our Culture's War on the American Family* (Grand Rapids, MI: Zondervan, 2024).

79. Ayaan Hirsi Ali, "Forced Reality | Ayaan Hirsi Ali LIVE at the Freedom Conference at the Reagan Ranch," broadcast November 15, 2025, Young America's Foundation, YouTube video, 1:05:50, https://www.youtube.com/watch?v=RI-HkkLZziL8

80. Thomas Sowell, *The Vision of the Anointed: Self-Congratulation as a Basis for Social Policy* (New York: Basic Books, 1995).

81. Thomas Sowell's Official Website, https://www.tsowell2.com (accessed December 11, 2025).

82. *Collected Works of Milton Friedman*, "Milton Friedman Digital Collections," Hoover Institution Library & Archives, Stanford University, accessed December 11, 2025, https://miltonfriedman.hoover.org/collections; Milton Friedman, *Free to Choose: A Personal Statement* (New York: Harcourt Brace Jovanovich, 1980).

83. Peter Santenello, "Inside America's Corruption Capital—Washington D.C." YouTube video, 1:13:50, June 22, 2024, https://www.youtube.com/watch?v=HQDdnZ__yTk

84. Civil Service Reform Act of 1978, 5 U.S.C. §§ 1101–7703; Merit Systems Protection Board, authority and functions, 5 U.S.C. § 1201.

85. PragerU, "The Bigger the Government..." | 5 Minute Videos, March 3, 2014, YouTube video, 5:17, https://www.youtube.com/watch?v=qr638pCfPxs

86. Whitney Alyse Webb, *One Nation Under Blackmail*, vols. 1–2.

87. Antony Davies, "Prof. Antony Davies: Why Government Fails, Explained," YouTube video, October 9, 2017, 1:18:02, at 1:42, https://www.youtube.com/watch?v=xxmXeLEcs9s

88. Helen Pluckrose and James Lindsay, *Cynical Theories: How Activist Scholarship Made Everything about Race, Gender, and Identity—and Why This Harms Everybody* (Durham, NC: Pitchstone Publishing, 2020).

89. Yuri Bezmenov, "FULL INTERVIEW with Yuri Bezmenov: The Four Stages of Ideological Subversion" (1984), interview by G. Edward Griffin, August 22, 2020, video, 1:21:28, YouTube, https://www.youtube.com/watch?v=yErKTVdETpw

90. Robert E. Rector et al., *The Harmful Effects of Early Sexual Activity and Multiple Sexual Partners Among Women: A Book of Charts* (Washington, DC: The Heritage Foundation, June 23, 2003).

91. Jordan B. Peterson, "Gay Marriage, Surrogacy, Divorce & Hookup Culture | Katy Faust | EP 527," YouTube video, 1:34:00, March 6, 2025, posted by The Dr. Jordan B. Peterson Podcast, https://www.youtube.com/watch?v=Q4Q0WXBH0HM&t=2031s

92. Katy Faust, *ThemBeforeUs.com*, accessed December 11, 2025, https://thembeforeus.com.

93. Joshua Philipp, "Trump Suggests Migration Is a Political Weapon Against America," *Crossroads with Joshua Philipp*, YouTube video, 1:05:07, https://www.youtube.com/watch?v=wZY6OIWdGU8&t=900s; Peter Schweizer, *The Invisible Coup: How American Elites and Foreign Powers Use Immigration as a Weapon* (New York: Harper, 2026), January 20, 2026, hardcover, https://www.amazon.com/Invisible-Coup-American-Foreign-Immigration/dp/0063422506/.

94. Roy Beck, *World Poverty, Immigration and Gumballs*; and GBNews, "EXPOSED: The Cloward-Piven STRATEGY Unleashed in the WEST!" YouTube video, 10:52, June 5, 2025, https://www.youtube.com/watch?v=Mp1Pk1QPuUQ

95. Tom Jefferson et al., "Physical Interventions to Interrupt or Reduce the Spread of Respiratory Viruses," *Cochrane Database of Systematic Reviews* 2023, no. 1 (2023): CD006207, https://doi.org/10.1002/14651858.CD006207.pub6

96. *Shout Your Abortion*. Accessed November 30, 2025. https://shoutyourabortion.com

97. The Officer Tatum Show. "Teachers FORCE Students Into School PRIDE Parade," YouTube video, posted June 6, 2023. https://www.youtube.com/watch?v=_Z_HwrTOldY

98. Jordan B. Peterson, "The Wounds That Won't Heal | Detransitioner Chloe Cole | EP 319," YouTube video, 2:01:36, January 2, 2023, https://youtu.be/6O3MzPeomqs

99. Boston Children's Hospital, "Center for Gender Health," accessed November 30, 2025, https://www.childrenshospital.org/programs/center-gender-health

100. Susan Morse, "Hospital and Physician Groups Ask DOJ to Investigate Threats to Gender-Affirming Care," *Healthcare Finance*, October 10, 2022, 4:54 p.m.

101. The Thinking Conservative News. "Judge Ketanji Brown Jackson Asked To Define a Woman." YouTube video, posted March 23, 2022. https://www.youtube.com/watch?v=UwtimpgJ-IQ

102. Mike Rowe, "Examining the Lia Thomas 'Incident' with Riley Gaines | *The Way I Heard It with Mike Rowe*," YouTube video, posted July 31, 2024. https://www.youtube.com/watch?v=bYkvEyLECd8

103. Alice Giordano, "YMCA Bans 80-Year-Old Who Confronted Male in Women's Shower Room," *The Epoch Times*, August 18, 2022, https://www.theepochtimes.com/us/ymca-bans-80-year-old-who-confronted-male-in-womens-shower-room-4673252

104. Kirk Cameron, *As You Grow* (El Paso, TX: Brave Books, 2022).

105. "Kirk Cameron Blocked From Reading His New Children's Book by More Than 50 Libraries," *New Guard*, July 19, 2023, by New Guard Staff and Carter Fortman.

106. Maia Kobabe, *Gender Queer: A Memoir* (Portland, OR: Oni Press, 2019).

107. "UK Arrests Over Social Media Posts Against Mass Immigration," *JRE Clips*, October 8, 2025, excerpt from *Joe Rogan Experience* #2390 with Jack Carr, YouTube video, https://www.youtube.com/watch?v=6XMPC1i78N0

108. The White House, *Build Back Better Framework*, August 13, 2025, White House Archives, https://bidenwhitehouse.archives.gov/build-back-better/

109. Forbes Breaking News. "MERCILESS: Citizen After Citizen Ruthlessly Confronts Mayor Johnson At Chicago City Council Meeting." YouTube video, posted December 17, 2024. https://www.youtube.com/watch?v=Eu1IQiRDKrI&t=86s

110. U.S. Department of Education, Institute of Education Sciences, National Center for Education Statistics, "NAEP Mathematics: State Achievement-Level Results, Grade 8," The Nation's Report Card, accessed November 30, 2025, https://www.nationsreportcard.gov/mathematics/states/achievement/?grade=8

111. "NAEP Report Card: Mathematics, National Achievement-Level Results — Grade 8," National Center for Education Statistics (US Department of Education), accessed December 4, 2025, https://www.nationsreportcard.gov/mathematics/nation/achievement/?grade=8

112. Michael Brendan. "If America Spends More Than Most Countries Per Student, Then Why Are Its Schools So Bad?" Business Insider, January 7, 2012.

113. The Rubin Report, "Evergreen State College Racism Controversy | Bret Weinstein | ACADEMIA," YouTube video, May 30, 2017, https://www.youtube.com/watch?v=-fEAPcgxnyY

114. Foundation for Individual Rights and Expression (FIRE), "Free Speech Zones," FIRE Research & Learn, accessed November 30, 2025, https://www.thefire.org/research-learn/free-speech-zones

115. Viktor Kravchenko, *I Chose Freedom: The Personal and Political Life of a Soviet Official* (New York: Charles Scribner's Sons, 1946).

116. Herbert Marcuse, "Repressive Tolerance," in *A Critique of Pure Tolerance*, by Robert Paul Wolff, Barrington Moore Jr., and Herbert Marcuse (Beacon Press, 1965).

117. TortureArchive, "The Most Horrifying Acts Islamic Caliphates Did to Slaves," YouTube video, 1:13:15, July 25, 2025, https://www.youtube.com/watch?v=_dro4zlGrzk&t=5s

118. Michael Knowles, "I Was Given to a Man When I Was a Child | Michael & The Sharia Survivor | Sabatina James," YouTube video, *The Michael*

119 Ayaan Hirsi Ali, "Female Genital Mutilation & 'Islamophobia' (Pt. 3)," interview by Dave Rubin, *The Rubin Report*, YouTube video, May 9, 2017, https://www.youtube.com/watch?v=CehgOCJzwZw&t=756s

120 Bel Trew, "Egypt's Sexual Assault Epidemic: Women at Egypt's Protests Often Must Fight More than the Political Cause That Brought Them into the Streets," *Al Jazeera*, August 14, 2013, https://www.aljazeera.com/features/2013/8/14/egypts-sexual-assault-epidemic

121 Jelena Andelkovic, "Bacha Bazi—Severe Child Abuse Disguised as an Afghani Custom," *Humanium*, September 13, 2022, https://www.humanium.org/en/bacha-bazi-severe-child-abuse-disguised-as-an-afghani-custom/

122 Ayaan Hirsi Ali, *Prey: Immigration, Islam, and the Erosion of Women's Rights* (New York: Harper, 2021).

123 Clay Risen, *Red Scare: Blacklists, McCarthyism, and the Making of Modern America* (New York: Scribner, 2025).

124 Jordan B. Peterson, "Jordan Peterson, God, & Christianity | Kaczor & Petrusek | EP 212," YouTube video, 2:03:18, December 27, 2021 (at 1:46:00), https://www.youtube.com/watch?v=m9Njk8vpToQ

125 Peter Robinson, "Mathematical Challenges to Darwin's Theory of Evolution" (interview with David Berlinski, David H. Gelernter, and Stephen C. Meyer), Hoover Institution, YouTube video, July 22, 2019, https://www.youtube.com/watch?v=noj4phMT9OE

126 Stephen C. Meyer, *Darwin's Doubt: The Explosive Origin of Animal Life and the Case for Intelligent Design* (New York: HarperOne, 2013).

127 Jordan B. Peterson, "Ancient Wisdom at an Ancient Library," lecture at Ralston College, YouTube video, 1:04:53, posted December 25, 2022, 00:46:58, https://www.youtube.com/watch?v=9ByjCwumwBM

128 Chris Harrison, *BibleViz* (visualization of Bible cross-references), accessed January 11, 2026, https://www.chrisharrison.net/index.php/Visualizations/BibleViz

129 Brandon Tatum, "Teachers FORCE Students Into School PRIDE Parade," *The Officer Tatum*, YouTube video, 8:09, June 6, 2023, https://www.youtube.com/watch?v=_Z_HwrTOldY

130 John F. Kennedy, remarks at a breakfast meeting with business leaders, Fort Worth, TX, November 14, 1963, in *Public Papers of the Presidents of the United States: John F. Kennedy*, 1963 (Washington, DC: Government Printing Office, 1964), 820.

131 G. Edward Griffin, *The Creature from Jekyll Island: A Second Look at the Federal Reserve*, 5th ed. (Westlake Village, CA: American Media, 2010); Ron Paul, *End the Fed* (New York: Grand Central Publishing, 2009).

132 Milton Friedman, *Free to Choose*, YouTube video playlist, uploaded by chuan, accessed September 27, 2025, https://www.youtube.com/playlist?list=PLt27IKoC5LS4wbD-28Jkv95UUm9H7wbVO4&si=Q9dJB-7NdSj0r6TQ9

133 Thomas Sowell, *Charter Schools and Their Enemies* (New York: Basic Books, 2020).

134 Jordan B. Peterson, "Educate Your Children! | Jeff Sandefer | EP 336," *The Jordan B. Peterson Podcast*, YouTube video, March 2, 2023, 2:00:38, https://www.youtube.com/watch?v=-FEUjcRWfu3c&list=PL8EZz_Jhi6Furglvf-rO-XtnZlgChCvNq&index=61; Acton Academy, One-Room Schoolhouses for the 21st Century, accessed December 5, 2025, https://www.actonacademy.org.

135 Jordan B. Peterson, "A Message From the Strictest Headmistress in the UK | Katharine Birbalsingh | EP 458," The Dr. Jordan B. Peterson Podcast, YouTube video, 1:31:03, June 24, 2024, https://www.youtube.com/watch?v=qs0s9kTFE5Y&t=318s; Michaela Community School, "Welcome to Michaela," accessed December 5, 2025, https://michaela.education

136 Jubilee, and PBD Podcast. "1 Capitalist vs 20 Anti-Capitalists (ft. Patrick Bet-David)," YouTube video, 1:43:36, August 31, 2025. https://www.youtube.com/watch?v=cwSXDr7XkNc&t=4979s

137 *The Pelican Brief*, directed by Alan J. Pakula (Burbank, CA: Warner Bros., 1993), film.

138 Sharyl Attkisson, *The Smear: How Shady Political Operatives and Fake News Control What You See, What You Think, and How You Vote* (New York: Harper, 2017); Sharyl Attkisson, *Slanted: How the News Media Taught Us to Love Censorship and Hate Journalism* (New York: Harper, 2020).

139 "The Great Global Warming Swindle—Full Documentary HD," produced by Wisdom Land, YouTube video, 1:13:25, August 19, 2018, https://www.youtube.com/watch?v=oYhCQv5tNsQ&t=73s

140 John Cook et al., "Quantifying the Consensus on Anthropogenic Global Warming in the Scientific Literature," *Environmental Research* Letters 8, no. 2 (2013): 024024, https://doi.org/10.1088/1748-9326/8/2/024024

141 Mark Lynas, Benjamin Z. Houlton, and Simon Perry, "Greater than 99% consensus on human caused climate change in the peer-reviewed scientific literature," *Environmental Research Letters* 16, no. 11 (November 2021): 114005, https://doi.org/10.1088/1748-9326/ac2966

142 Union Films, "The Communist Takeover Explained (1966)," YouTube video, 7:35, October 23, 2022, https://www.youtube.com/watch?v=I7zNy4gfx8U

143 Federal Bureau of Investigation, Crime Data Explorer: *Homicide Offenses, 2020* (Washington, DC: U.S. Department of Justice, 2020), https://cde.ucr.cjis.gov/LATEST/webapp/#/pages/explorer/crime/homicide

144 Paul Joseph Watson, "The Tragedy of Cultural Relativism," YouTube video, 6:56, December 24, 2018, https://www.youtube.com/watch?v=IUXteUGhh7w

145 Webhost, Inc. *2024 Annual Report*. https://s28.q4cdn.com/599997874/files/doc_financials/2024/ar/2024-Annual-Report-Webhost.pdf

146 "Map of the Voyages of Christopher Columbus, 1492-1504," *World History Encyclopedia*, accessed October 20, 2025, https://www.worldhistory.org/image/14653/map-of-the-voyages-of-christopher-columbus-1492-15/.

147 Glenn Beck, "Why ESG Is the Biggest Scam of the 21st Century | Vivek Ramaswamy | Ep 151," YouTube video, 1:29:05, October 22, 2024, https://www.youtube.com/watch?v=y16j2NGumqI

148 Michael Knowles, "Christopher Columbus, Hero Not Heathen | Michael Knowles LIVE at University of Notre Dame," Young America's Foundation, YouTube video, 1:05:11, October 2019, https://www.youtube.com/watch?v=8Y-Ag-ocB-Q

149 Martin Luther King Jr., "I Have a Dream," speech delivered August 28, 1963, Washington, D.C., National Archives.

150 Jordan B. Peterson, "Peddlers of Environmental Doom Have Shown Their True Totalitarian Colours: Corporations and Utopians Are Offering Authoritarian Solutions to Crises Only Democracy and Free Markets Can Solve," *The Telegraph*, August 15, 2022.

151 Yeonmi Park, *In Order to Live: A North Korean Girl's Journey to Freedom* (New York: Penguin Press, 2015).

152 Tim Pool, "From BLM To Trump Supporters, The Cartier Family | The Culture War with Tim Pool," YouTube video, streamed live October 18, 2024, 1:55:10, https://www.youtube.com/watch?v=PiUZo5AuPG0

153 *Real Time with Bill Maher*, "Elon Musk on the 'Woke Mind Virus' | Real Time with Bill Maher (HBO)," YouTube video, 14:53. April 28, 2023, https://www.youtube.com/watch?v=qFEaTk--tZo

154 Neil D. Fleming and Colleen Mills, "Not Another Inventory, Rather a Catalyst for Reflection," To Improve the Academy 11, no. 1 (1992): 137–155.

Thank you for your interest in the world we share.

Though the story of good vs. evil is still unfolding. Remember, our ending has been promised—and it is beautiful...

"He will wipe every tear from their eyes.
There will be no more death or mourning or crying or
pain, for the old order of things has passed away."
—*Revelation 21:4*

www.ingramcontent.com/pod-product-compliance
Lightning Source LLC
Chambersburg PA
CBHW042358030426
42337CB00032B/5148